William Bourne

Not Just Baseball

Traveling to Remote America

Not Just Baseball
TRAVELING TO REMOTE AMERICA

iUniverse books may be ordered through booksellers or by contacting:

iUniverse
1663 Liberty Drive
Bloomington, IN 47403
www.iuniverse.com
844-349-9409

ISBN: 978-1-6632-0131-7 (sc)
ISBN: 978-1-6632-0132-4 (e)

Library of Congress Control Number: 2020914796

Print information available on the last page.

iUniverse rev. date: 03/18/2021

NOT JUST BASEBALL

BASEBALL

Traveling to Remote America

WILLIAM BOURNE

INTRODUCTION

I have had a lifelong love affair with baseball, but I stumbled upon fascinating small-town America during these trips from the mid-1990s to 2019. Minor league baseball was the original focus, as I zeroed in on Class A–rated teams. I chose Class A because it would introduce us to attractive, remote small towns. There are four levels of the farm system: Rookie, Class A, Double-A, and Triple-A.

We traveled approximately 35,589 miles via airplanes and rented cars. We saw forty-five games in twenty-two states, plus Western Canada. We always traveled in July or August and therefore decided that the southern states were just too hot. Seattle was our westernmost point, and Portland, Maine, was the easternmost.

Once we moved away from both coasts, we found the people to be very patriotic and friendly in these remote, quaint towns. It was easy to meet the local people, which made the trips even more interesting.

One of my rules was to sit at the counters of the local eateries. Preferably, there would be two seats between two locals and pickup trucks parked outside. Fast-food restaurants were verboten.

Superhighways were not used the majority of the time because they would not take us into the small towns. One country road in Upstate New York introduced us to a turtle race on Main Street one Saturday morning.

Brother Jim accompanied me on every trip except the last two. Son Michael joined us on four trips, including the last one, to Spokane, Washington, and northwestern Montana. My future son-in-law, Chase Millard, drove all one thousand miles to accompany us on our upper–New England journey. My encouraging wife, Odessa, joined us on the last trip. All the games started in the afternoon or early evening, and we were impulsive travelers/tourists during the day. Nothing was planned. Everything was spontaneous.

We twice visited Montana, the fourth-largest state, for the first time in 2001, when we visited the eastern and north-central part. The second time, in 2019, we visited the northwestern section. We could easily return to Montana for two or three more trips because there was so much to see there.

The major league teams owned and controlled the players and their contracts. They owned all the baseball equipment, including the baseballs and bats. They could even depreciate the players. The stadiums were usually owned by the municipalities. Local shop owners came to offer entertainment to lure people to the park to spend money, tossing hotdogs into the stands, playing rock and roll music, and having young kids race around the bases in between innings. Dancing in the aisles, fireworks, and skydivers were all part of the fun evening.

Barnes and Noble had a map that listed every minor league team in America, Canada, and Mexico. It was very helpful in determining the direction of our next journey and the actual miles we were to drive. As a result, we would often stumble upon something interesting in a remote part of a given state. For instance, we once turned to the McNally map as we were crossing northern Illinois. We saw Ulysses Grant's house in Galena, Illinois, just south of Dubuque, Iowa. The house was somewhat simple, but I was still inspired to read his biography. A similar experience occurred when we were exposed to Mark Twain's youth in Hannibal, Missouri. This led to reading three of his novels plus a 627-page biography. Needless to say, he was one interesting human being.

In this book, I wish to educate people about baseball and the quaint hamlets and villages tucked into remote corners in several of our fifty states. In July 2010, we encircled Pittsburgh for four days, seeing several attractive suburban towns. Twenty years after the steel industry broke down completely, Pittsburgh reinvented itself in a regeneration of new skills in research, health care, and software.

In 2019, the major leagues made a proposal to eliminate forty-two minor league teams. Twenty-eight of the forty-two teams are either Rookie level or short-season Class A ball. Nine Appalachian League teams on the list averaged 1,072 fans per game in 2019, including six teams averaging under one thousand. The only team in the league not on the cut list is the Yankee affiliate in Pulaski, Virginia, whose 2,821 average attendance topped the Appalachian in 2019. There are four Double-A teams on the cut list: Chattanooga and Jackson in the Southern League, plus Binghamton and Erie in the Eastern League.

Nostalgia hit me as I concluded the writing of the book. The last trip to Spokane, Washington, was chosen to research my father's five years in Gonzaga Boarding School in 1917–1922. And then we drove to Helena, Montana, to do research at the Montana Historical Society Library, but this time it was for my grandfather, who was a state senator for two terms in the early 1900s. I felt the warm connection with my forefathers, having enjoyed the journeys and the privilege to write about them.

CHAPTER 1
NOT JUST BASEBALL

St. Paul's Episcopal Church, on Chapel Lane, in Riverside, Connecticut, had a hardball team entered in the Greenwich Recreation Board summer league for eighteen years and under. I played on the team with my brothers, Jim and Sonny, for a few years in the 1950s. Jim was a second baseman, Sonny a catcher, and I a pitcher. One memorable evening at Binney Park in Old Greenwich, I was the starting pitcher against the league leading the St. Catherine's team. They were ahead 2 to 0 in the sixth inning when Dick Giansello came up to bat. He was the star quarterback for Greenwich High School football team. At six foot three and 230 pounds, he was unquestionably one of the best athletes in the school. My brother ran in from second base and asked me, "How are you going to pitch to this guy?" He claimed many years later that I said, "I'm going to throw him a high hard one."

I replied, "No way could I have said that because I never had a high hard one."

A few minutes later, my next pitch was deposited over the Binney Park Department house in deep left-center field onto the road some 440 feet away from home plate.

I also pitched for the Iona Prep School varsity team in New Rochelle, New York, and had one incident that I will never forget. The coach sent me in to relieve in one of the middle innings with the bases loaded and no outs. The first batter went down swinging, the second batter also struck out, and I had a 0-and-2 count on the third hitter. I threw a roundhouse curveball, which I aimed at his front shoulder, and it broke right over the heart of the plate for a called third strike. The batter was frozen. I was walking off the field toward our bench as my teammates jumped up and down with excitement. I was so pumped up, until the coach walked over to me and said, "You should have wasted that pitch with a 0-and-2 count. How can you throw a pitch right over the center of the plate with the bases loaded?"

Needless to say, he was right, but it was disappointing to hear, as I was still excited by the fact that I had struck out all three batters and no runs had been scored.

As Catholics, we attended St. Catherine's Grammar School in Riverside. I pitched on the grammar school team, coached by Frank Santora, a retired postman. He told the whole team, "Stick with me. I will put you up in the majors." Frank also told all of us to take the first two pitches and then hit to right. Most of us were right-handed hitters, so we were usually late in swinging anyway, and more often than not, if we made contact, the ball would end up in right field. At age thirteen, I preferred to play for the Episcopal team, St. Paul's in the summer league. My two brothers, ages fifteen and sixteen, were already playing there.

Father Ganley, pastor of St. Catherine's Church, came to our house that summer to express his dislike to our father about his three boys playing on the Episcopal team. Seeing that most of our friends were on the St. Paul's team, we had no interest in joining the St. Catherine's team. Our father threatened to cease donating to the church and asked the priest to leave our home.

Our practice field was at the Riverside Grammar School diamond. We all loved the game so much that we would practice every evening of the summer if there was not a league game. It became our *Field of Dreams*.

During the Korean War, my two older brothers served in the US Army in South Korea and Germany. I was left in charge of cutting our lawn every weekend. Our property consisted of six acres and one pond, with four acres of lawn. One Sunday afternoon, I was cutting the lawn with a gasoline-fired triple Locke lawnmower, which had two additions to make the overall cut more than seventy inches. Of course, I walked behind this unit for several hours every weekend, but this day, it just so happened that the Yankees were on television playing a double header. So, every hour or so, I would take a break to watch the game in our cellar near where the mower was stored. After most inning breaks, Mel Allen, the Yankees announcer, would start his commercial pitch for Balantine Beer—purity, body, and flavor—then reach to his right to open a small refrigerator, where there were several cans of Balantine, and he would crack one open. Well, this procedure continued throughout the afternoon and into the early evening, when the refrigerator appeared to have only a few cans remaining. Come 7:30 p.m., in the eighth inning of the second game, I had just about finished cutting the lawn. I was back in the TV room when a commercial came on. Mel, speaking with a bit of a slur, opened the refrigerator only to find it empty. Then there was a musical interlude from the TV studio.

In retrospect, what wonderful summers we had in Riverside, Connecticut, riding our bikes one mile every evening at ages thirteen to sixteen to practice and play simulated innings from 6:00 p.m. until 8:30 p.m. Otto Bear Albinus was our coach, assisted by his son, Jack. Bear was a tireless coach who pitched batting practice for at least one hour. He was a fifty-five-year-old man, with broad, muscular shoulders, and he threw a straight overhand fastball. Then he would hit ground balls to all the infielders. Jack was tall and lanky. He would work with the outfielders, pitchers, and catchers. Jack was invited to a tryout in the minor leagues. After a two-year stint, he returned home and became our head coach.

Ada's

Our reward after practice was either a chocolate sundae or a vanilla milkshake at Ada's Candy Store, also known as the Louise Shop or the Louse House. It was located on Riverside Avenue, near the railroad station. It had a porch in front where we all hung out. Ada and her older sister, Louise, had run the store since the mid-1950s. Ada made a point of remembering our names. She loved us all and was our fairy godmother. Jim and I drove to her store in the mid-1990s to tell Ada that we were organizing a reunion from the 1950s, and she was definitely invited. Having not been in the store for at least twenty-five years, we walked in and said to Ada, "You have to guess who we are." She looked us over for a few minutes, gave a slight pause, and said, "The Bourne Boys." How did she remember us after so many years? She loved and remembered every one of us. We were her adopted children.

Ada was reluctant to agree to attend our reunion. I told her she had been an integral part of our younger years. I had a car and driver take her to and from the party at the Riverside Yacht Club only half a mile away. More than a hundred old friends attended, including Ada, who enjoyed herself so much that she was one of the last to leave.

Fast-forward the story to August 1994, when I decided to relive our baseball-playing days by convincing Jim to attend a few minor league games in Upstate New York and Massachusetts. Jim was two years and seven months older and was entering Notre Dame as a freshman in 1951 so we did not hang around together too much back in those days. So, this was an opportunity to come closer as brothers, watching the game we grew up to love.

Oneonta

Oneonta, New York, was about 170 miles from Greenwich, Connecticut. We drove through the beautiful Catskill Mountains, taking a circuitous route by way of Greenville, New York, to visit with Ginger Hoyt Cantarella, a very old friend of ours from Phillipsburg, New Jersey. Even at age seven, Jim had had a crush on her and her beautiful red hair. Ginger was an accomplished artist who had a charming studio in her barn behind the house. We met her husband, Herman Shonbrun, who was a walking dictionary and encyclopedia wrapped in one, though he did not play baseball. His paper route as a young boy was in Tampa, Florida, where he delivered the morning paper to the Cincinnati Reds' spring training team. That sparked his interest in baseball. He told me he had joined the army at age sixteen, during World War 2, then went to college on the GI Bill, studying theater. He came to Manhattan and became one of the original founders of Circle in the Square. He moved to Brooklyn and became a die-hard Dodgers fan. Even though I was a true-blue Yankee fan, I invited Herman to join us for the rest of the baseball trip. Unfortunately, this erudite man declined because he was feeling under the weather. We eventually arrived in Oneonta, located halfway between Albany and Binghamton. This was the home of the National Soccer Hall of Fame, Hartwick College, and Sunny College, but we were there to see the Oneonta Yankees baseball team.

The Oneonta Yankees played in the New York-Penn League at Damaschke Field, which was built in 1914. Oneonta is the smallest city in the league and the fourth-smallest city of the more than two hundred communities in organized baseball. The New York-Penn League was formed in 1939 and was originally called the Pony League, as the member clubs were from Pennsylvania, Ontario, and New York. More than 120 Oneonta players made it to "the show." A few names: Ken Brett, Roberto Kelly, Al Leiter, Jim Leyritz, Don Mattingly, J. T. Snow, and Bernie Williams. Buck Showalter's first managerial job was here in 1985. John Elway, fresh out of Stanford University, was a pitcher in 1982 for the Oneonta Yanks.

In the official program, August 16, 1994, there was an article about inflation entitled, "Back When a Dollar Was Worth 100 Cents":

	1939	1994	e. 2016
Aspirin 100 tablets	9c	$6.89	$7.59
Tooth Polish	28c	$2.89	$5.90
Florida oranges (one dozen)	22c	$1.44	$4.80
Eggs (one dozen)	12c	$0.99	$3.99
Pepsi bottles (6 pack)	25c	$2.75	$4.59
Golf Shoes	$6.50	$68.00	$170.00

The Oneonta Yankees bring more than $1 million annually into the local economy. The total attendance comes to about 56,000 fans per year, or 1,435 per game.

A half hour before the game started, we had a beer in a local joint next to the ball field. The bartender, along with a few locals, preferred to talk about NFL football, so we departed for the game. The major league parks were closed due to a players' strike. While big-league parks like Yankee Stadium, Camden Yards, and Comisky Park remained dark over the weekend, minor league parks like Damaschle Field, in the foothills of the Catskills, abounded with pitchers hurling, hitters swinging, runners flying, managers jawing, umpires emoting, and fans cheering, booing, and downing hot dogs, soft drinks, and a local powdered pastry called fried dough.

The Yankees top draft pick that season, Brian Buchanan, was out of the University of Virginia. He was a tall, strapping six-foot-four, 220-pound right fielder. He doubled in the second inning, and the public address announcer told us that he had "won a sub of his choice at Subway on Main Street in Oneonta." When Buchanan tripled in the sixth, he again won a sub of his choice in addition to a free "wash, cut, and blow dry at Rodrac's Hair in Motion, on Main Street. The Oneonta Yanks beat the Welland Pirates 8 to 3, roughing up their pitcher, Kane Davis, who had an Earned Run Average of 1.99, the second best in the New York-Penn League. The players filed off the field, and the fans filed out of the ballpark. Soon the old ballpark was dark, like Yankee Stadium. The next day, however, there would be another game in Damaschle Field.

At breakfast the next morning, in the local diner, we met the head of maintenance of Damaschle Field, who invited us to visit the baseball diamond, of which he was very proud. In the clubhouse, he told us about his wife's sudden passing. When he heard about it, George Steinbrenner sent up two dozen roses, which classified him as "a classy guy." My brother and I remained silent because although we were very loyal Yankee fans, we were not fond of Mr. Steinbrenner.

Pittsfield

We then packed our bags and headed east toward Pittsfield, Massachusetts, to see the Pittsfield Mets. Traveling on backroads through Albany County, we drove over the Hudson River and made our way to New Lebanon, New York, via State Route 20. We toured the Shaker Museum and buildings. The primary settlement was established in New Lebanon in 1861. The Shakers are a Christian religious group that originated in Great Britain around 1750. The Shakers were originally known as the Shaking Quakers, because they commonly trembled in religious fervor in their services. The museum's holdings span over 180 years, related to all aspects of the American Shakers. More than 80 percent was acquired directly from Shaker communities. The furniture was simple and functional. We wondered how long this community could last if celibacy was one of the rules of the Shaker religion.

A half hour later we arrived in Pittsfield at Wahconah Park in time to see the Pittsfield Mets play the Utica Blue Sox. Our general admission tickets were $2.75 per person. The stands are right on top of the right- and left-field lines, which means there is virtually no foul territory. At the end of the third inning, all the players left the field as usual, and all the fans went behind the stands to reload their orders of hot dogs and refreshments. The other team did not send their players onto the field, so Jim and I looked at each other and said, "Where did everybody go?"

Welcome to Wahconah Park's famous sun delay, an event that is unique in minor league baseball. Built facing west in 1919, before the advent of night baseball, Wahconah Park maintains old-fashioned minor league charm as the sun sets over the left-center-field fence. On certain evenings, when the bright sun sets, it shines directly into the batter's, catcher's, and umpire's eyes, causing the delay, which lasted about fifteen minutes.

Norman Rockwell

The cover of the program was a famous painting by Norman Rockwell entitled *Game Called Because of Rain*. It was first published on the cover of the *Saturday Evening Post* on April 23, 1949. Depicted is a game between the Brooklyn Dodgers and the Pittsburgh Pirates at Ebbets Field, with the Pirates leading 1–0. the umpires have to make a tough call, looking at the dark sky and feeling the drops of rain. There were a few baseball quips and quotes in the program:

- Jim Bouton: "Baseball players are smarter than football players. How often do you see a baseball team penalized for having too many men on the field?"
- Larry Anderson: "Why is the ball FAIR when it hits the FOUL pole?"
- Casey Stengel: "All right, everyone line up alphabetically according to your height."
- Yogi Berra: Yogi was asked if he wanted his pizza cut into four or eight slices. "Better make it four. I don't think I can eat eight."

The Pittsfield Mets defeated the Utica Blue Sox 6–1, a one-sided game that was not very exciting. It appeared that the pitchers overpowered the hitters, as virtually nobody pulled the ball. More interesting was watching the children running out on the field and dancing during the fifth inning.

The next morning, we drove several miles down Route 7 to Stockbridge to tour the Norman Rockwell Museum. The exhibition included more than 150 works by contemporary illustrators who created their own versions of oversized baseball cards. The main gallery of the museum featured Rockwell's originals *Game Called Because of Rain* and *Hundredth Year of Baseball*, on loan this summer from National Baseball Hall of Fame and Museum in Cooperstown, New York.

Norman Rockwell brought baseball illustration to wide and diverse audiences on the covers of the *Saturday Evening Post*. Norman Rockwell and baseball are a natural combination. These two

American institutions have a lot in common: nostalgia for days gone by and the telling of stories and reflections of history in the making. In a career spanning more than sixty years, Rockwell chronicled major moments of the twentieth century, always painting ordinary people as heroic champions of day-to-day existence. Children, family values, and small towns were all common subjects for America's favorite illustrator. One of my favorite nonbaseball scenes is the painting of a ten-year-old boy running away from home, looking up at a policeman who is sitting on a stool at a counter in a diner. I bought a copy, which I gave to my son years later when he himself became a cop in eastern Ohio.

Norman Rockwell was born in New York City in 1894. Having always wanted to be an artist, Norman left high school to study art at the National Academy of Design. He painted his first commission of four Christmas cards before his sixteenth birthday. At age twenty-one, Rockwell's family moved to New Rochelle, New York, where Norman set up a studio with the cartoonist Clyde Forsythe and produced work for such magazines as *Life*, *Literary Digest*, and *Country Gentlemen*. In 1916, the twenty-two-year-old Rockwell painted his first cover for the *Saturday Evening Post*. Over the next forty-seven years, another 321 Rockwell covers would appear on the *Post*. In 1930, he married for the second time, schoolteacher Mary Barstow, and the couple had three sons. The family moved to Arlington, Vermont, in 1939, and Rockwell's work began to reflect small-town American life. In 1953, the Rockwell family moved to Stockbridge, Massachusetts in 1977, Rockwell received the nation's highest civilian honor, the Presidential Medal of Freedom.

CHAPTER 2

MICHAEL JORDAN ET AL.: WEIRD STORIES IN BASEBALL

Minor league baseball bears about the same relationship to the major league variety as a real show of *Cats* in Paducah bears to the real thing on Broadway. The game retains a small-town, small-time flavor. The owners, keen to squeeze every penny out of their businesses, run promotions like pie-eating contests, on-field baseball-throwing contests, tricycle races, pizza giveaways, cheerleading exhibitions, bingo games, skydivers, and drawings for a free oil change. The stadiums are usually owned by the municipalities, and the players are depreciated by the major league teams. The negatives facing the players: terrible travel conditions, questionable living conditions, and low pay for seasonal work. Defeat has to be part of their makeup: good teams lose one out of three games; good hitters make an out seven times every ten at bats. But the ultimate goal or dream is to reach the major leagues.

There is, however, one small cost that all baseball leagues have on their books, which is not known to the public: baseball mud. There was a coach for the Philadelphia Athletics in the 1930s, Lena Blackburne, who introduced a special mud. At the time, baseballs came with a factory gloss. Pitchers couldn't grip it easily, so they applied shoe polish, tobacco juice, and dirt. Lena brought some mud from his home in Palmyra, New Jersey, about ten miles northeast of downtown Philadelphia. Soon, all the American League was using it. There is a farm located on a small creek off the Delaware River. You more or less skim the sediment off the top of the riverbank with a shovel. The Army Corps of Engineers did a study and found a high content of feldspar, which is just fine enough to remove the gloss without scratching the leather at all. Rawlings once tried to replicate the mud but couldn't do it. For spring training, each major league team gets one three-pound container for fifty dollars. Then, in February, one is shipped to each home park. Minor league teams have to find local riverbanks to get their own mud.

Pitcher Justin Verlander of the Houston Astros said the baseballs used in the 2017 World Series were a "little slick." A slicker baseball is harder to grip and control, and the slider may not break as much. Verlander said there is a different feel to the grain of the baseball.

From the batter's viewpoint, they have been complaining in the past two years, 2018 and 2019, that too much dirt rubbed onto the baseball prevents the batter from seeing the seams as well. Whenever a pitcher throws a ball into the dirt, known as spiking the ball, the catcher flicks it immediately over to a ball boy near the dugout. No conversation between catcher and umpire. Automatically, he gets a new one from the umpire and throws it to the pitcher. This appears to be an unwritten rule.

My son-in-law, Chase Millard, feels that stealing first base is an interesting proposal because the pitcher has a big advantage when the count goes to 0 and 2 or 1 and 2. He spikes the next pitch, which is not blocked by the catcher, and goes to the backstop. The batter can then attempt to steal first base.

Mike Vaccaro of the *New York Post* once wrote, "Sure, baseball on its own is supposed to take your mind off things—troubles with the boss, arguments with the spouse, the craziness of the political campaigns, bills and debts and balloon payments. Crack open a beer, crush a hot dog, kick back, relax and enjoy." Of course, you do come to the ballpark to see your team win. Vaccaro also wrote, "Winning is satisfying. Winning feels better than losing. Winning makes the summer last a little bit longer."

Each major league team is allowed one class Double-A team and one Triple-A team, and most have a handful of Class A teams, which are often the first step for new players. The team rosters in Class A change every season, which makes managing so difficult. A player finds his groove and is promoted to Double-A. It is very rare for a player to skip the minors and go straight to the major leagues. Many of the players come directly from high school. More come from junior college and college, but many more today are arriving from the Dominican Republic, Venezuela, and the Caribbean islands. Several of the sunny colleges are producing better players, but most rookies have to reluctantly experience "riding the bus" in the Class A leagues.

There are 160 teams in the minor leagues, which are in every state except Alaska, Hawaii, and Wyoming. Alaska has one team in the college league, and there are several leagues known as independent leagues, which do not have any official links to major league baseball. These leagues also go by the nicknames the "farm system," the "farm club," or "farm teams" because of a joke passed around by major league players in the 1930s, when St. Louis Cardinals' general manager, Branch Richey, formalized the system. He said teams in small towns were "growing players down on the farm like corn." However, startlingly, only one out of fourteen players make it to "the show." Due to financial losses, forty-two teams in the minor leagues will lose their affiliations with major league teams in 2021.

The minors afford a glimpse of baseball's greats before they're great. The talent varies wildly, but it is a cheap Saturday afternoon to entertain your family at the local park. In 1993, attendance was at an all-time high of 30 million. In 2014, it was 42,411,194, an increase of 41 percent, even though football and its violence have captured the attention of the American people.

Michael Jordan

I know the newspapers have to cover the strike. Major league baseball was faced with a walkout later in the year 1994, which also annulled the World Series. Then, the beginning of the 1995 season was postponed for a short period. But back in New York City, I was reading about Michael Jordan retiring from basketball at age thirty-one and signing with the Chicago White Sox baseball team, who assigned him to the AA Birmingham Barons as an outfielder, managed by Terry Francona. Francona managed the Boston Red Sox to a World Series title a decade later. In the Grapefruit League that winter, Michael went 3 for 20, or 0.150. Manager Francona said, "It is amazing that he went to AA after not playing since High School and stole 30 bases and drove in 44 runs."

At a news conference, Jordan said his father's death was not why he was leaving the NBA. "I have nothing more to prove in basketball," Jordan said. "I have no more challenges that I felt I could get motivated for. It doesn't have anything to do with media pressure, or anything other than that as I had achieved everything in basketball I could."

Jerry Reinsdorf, owner of the White Sox, was gushing with hope that Michael would be successful and eventually fill all the seats at Comiskey Park. Jerry flew to Birmingham several times to watch Jordan play. At his opening game, there was not a vacant seat as 10,359 fans rushed through the turnstiles to see Jordan. Also, 130 members of the media were in attendance. Michael said, "If I develop the skills to be up here, great. If I don't, at least I fulfilled a dream trying." He wore number 45 for the Barons, the number he wore for his Laney (North Carolina) High School baseball team.

The Barons set a home attendance record of 467,867 and pushed Southern League crowds past 2.5 million people. For several years following the 1994 season, Jordan's number 45 Barons jersey remained the most popular merchandise item. Arguably the best athlete of our day, he mastered one sport, professional basketball, and was now starting near the bottom of our national pastime, riding the team bus throughout the south. However, in 396 at-bats, he produced only a pair of home runs, a .192 batting average, and 44 runs batted in. But Jordan must have known in his heart of hearts that although he played minor league baseball, any .192 hitter who helped his team nearly double attendance at home and on the road was not a minor leaguer. He must have known that the dispute taking place in major league cities across the United States was not merely a baseball conflict but a labor issue that included most individual sports.

He was the most significant athlete of our time since Mohammad Ali, but he could not hit the curveball. His inability to succeed in the minor leagues verified my belief that hitting a baseball is one of the most difficult acts in sports. One is attempting to hit a round ball with a rounded bat. Think about that! And the fastball comes at you at ninety-five miles per hour. Yogi Berra said, "A batter cannot think and hit at the same time."

Ted Williams said, "Hitting a baseball is the hardest act in sports."

Most good hitters have 20/12 vision. And they have only milliseconds to process the image. It takes three hundred to four hundred milliseconds just to blink. And this is to say nothing of splitters and sliders.

The pitcher's mound is sixty feet and six inches from home plate, but he releases the ball when he is about fifty-five feet away. And the batter has half a second to decide whether to swing. Even if he has developed a trained swing, it is most definitely just a plain guess. It is all about timing and some luck. Perhaps the batter has to be superhuman.

Would Jordan have succeeded with a metal bat? We will never know the answer, but metal bats are still an issue today. The NCAA approved aluminum bats in 1974. Home run totals increased, and batting averages skyrocketed. Aluminum bats are better than wood bats because they provide more power, a faster swing, and a larger sweet spot. They are lighter by more than five ounces. The hardness and resilience of aluminum can result in much greater speeds when the ball comes off the bat. Wood bats provide hitters with better mechanics, better approach, and better contact, and they make the player a better hitter. However, wooden bats are prone to breaking on inside pitches. But safety is an issue for the pitcher and the third baseman, who have trouble defending a line drive right at them. A third baseman in the New Jersey Little League was killed instantly several years ago by a line drive to his chest.

The top-rated wooden bats are Barnett, Louisville Slugger Ash, Easton Pro Stix, Louisville Slugger Youth Bat, and Louisville Slugger Maple Bat.

Jordan did return to professional basketball after one year with the Birmingham Barons, and he helped the Chicago Bulls win three more NBA titles. He played fifteen seasons, won the scoring title ten times, and had a career average of 30.1 points per game, the most in NBA history.

Casey Stengel said back in the 1950s, "Every time you come to the ballpark, you will always see something different." Case in point: I was sitting near the right-field foul line in Yankee Stadium about thirty-five years ago when a squirrel climbed up the right field foul pole and sat on the top. During a recent game (June 2019) there was a red-tailed hawk sitting in a statuesque manner on top of one of the Yankee flag poles, looking down on all the fans without a care in the world.

Other Idiosyncrasies of Baseball

1. The Milwaukee Brewers and St. Louis Cardinals did something never done before in baseball. On April 3, 2018, the first two batters in the first inning hit home runs. The last two batters finished in the last inning with home runs to win the game.

2. Babe Ruth hit the longest home run ever hit while playing in an exhibition game of touring major leaguers in Birmingham, Alabama. His ball sailed over the outfield fence onto a freight train that did not stop until it reached Nashville, Tennessee, two hundred miles away.

3. Baseball is different from NFL games in a number of ways: First, there are no time clocks (one exception: pitchers). Second, there are different dimensions in each ballpark.

4. Midway Stadium, home of St. Paul, Minnesota Saints, has a pot-bellied pig carry baseballs from the dugout to the home-plate umpire. Massages and haircuts are given to fans in the stands.

5. A home-run hitter for the El Paso (Texas) Diablos trots around the bases but slows up between third base and home plate because there is a wall near the field where several dozen fans wait with a dollar bill in their hands to drop into the player's helmet. The player shakes hands with the fans, signs autographs, and chats it up with everybody. This bonding between player and fan is unique to baseball. This ritual started during the barnstorming days, when players counted on contributions as part of their pay.

6. Ken Singleton, broadcaster for the New York Yankees, said from the broadcasting booth on August 24, 2018, "There was a pitcher recently who asked the umpire for a clean ball. Umpire threw him a new ball, pitcher massaged it and then asked for another one. The umpire then rolled five clean balls on the grass out to the pitcher's mound."

7. Out of left field. Why is "left field" the spot where kooky ideas come from? In 1961, William Safire devoted a *NY Times* column to the topic, putting forth numerous ideas. A colorful explanation is that behind the ivy covered left-field wall at the Cubs' West Side Grounds, in use from 1893–1915, was a mental hospital whose patients could sometimes be heard making bizarre remarks during the game.

8. Why do so many terms come from baseball, horse racing, and boxing? Because these were the most popular sports in America in the first part of the twentieth century.

9. *NY Times* article about Bill Murphy (July 23, 2018). Murphy was nineteen when filming Ted Williams on his last day in the Majors. Williams hit a home run in the bottom of the eighth inning. He did not tip his hat to the fans. John Updike, who was at the game, wrote roughly a month later in the *New Yorker*, "Gods do not answer letters."

10. My sister, Alice Ryan, walked into our mother's bedroom when she was ninety-eight years old and a bit "around the bend." Mother said, "Billy is great! Did you know that about Billy?" "Yes," said Alice, "but what did he do?" Mother said, "You did not hear? He pitched a no-hitter for the Yankees in the World Series."

11. Umpire's position behind home plate. Take the slot. He stands right behind the shoulder of the catcher that is closest to the batter. This is the prescribed technique for all umps in calling balls and strikes. As my friend Mike Gilronan, former pitcher, liked to say, this is "getting in the slot."

12. What is the maximum number of pitches to one batter, during one official at-bat, not counting foul balls? The count goes to three balls and two strikes. There are two outs with a man on first base. The runner attempts to steal second base and is thrown out. The same batter leads off the next inning, and the count goes to three balls and two strikes, and he strikes out for a total of eleven pitches.

13. This is contributed by Joanne Duncanson, PT, in Vero Beach, Florida. The longest at-bat in the majors since such records began in 1988 was April 22, 2018, when Angels rookie right-hander Jamie Barria kept throwing strikes against the Giants' Brandon Belt, who kept fouling them off and fouling them off. Belt hit eleven consecutive balls into the crowd on a full count, hanging in for an epic twenty-one-pitch at-bat before lining out to right field. Belt said, "I wasn't going to give it up, and the pitcher wasn't either. It made for a good battle." In all, the left-handed Belt fouled off sixteen pitches, ending an at-bat that lasted more than twelve minutes. Later in the game, Belt homered to lead the Giants over the Angels.

14. A fan sitting near the right-field foul line, near the foul pole in the Miami Marlins stadium, in early September 2019, caught a fly ball hit his way. The same batter at the same at-bat hit another foul ball caught by the same man. There are no official statistics on fans catching balls in the stands, but this appears to be a first.

15. Chase rate: This is the percentage of times a batter swings at pitches that are outside the strike zone. Giancarlo Stanton, power hitter for the New York Yankees, watches this statistic very closely.

16. Jim Bouton, former American League pitcher, wrote a funny book about baseball: *Ball Four*. Some baseball trivia: a screwball can be a pitch or a person. Stealing is legal.

CHAPTER 3

UTICA, NEWARK, LARCHMONT, AND ELMIRA, NEW YORK

. . . .

An Accident on Long Island Sound

Back in Manhattan, I am wondering where we should go on our next minor league baseball trip. While writing this piece, I remember reading somewhere that the past is really almost as much a work of the imagination as the future. But unlike John Steinbeck's *Travels with Charlie*, I actually did take these trips with my brother. It was a way to relive our baseball playing days of the 1950s, flying to different sections of the country, renting a car to drive to dozens of Class A ballparks. It was revealed in 2012 that Steinbeck did not travel with his dog. His traveling mate was his wife.

Sports fans in New York City were still very upset about the major league baseball strike. The issues were as follows: (1) Most owners wanted an increase in revenue sharing, but the players wanted an increase also; (2) TV contracts; players wanted a piece of TV contracts (3) no more salary arbitration; (4) players' pensions and health benefits were to come out of players' half of revenues; and (5) players proposed a luxury tax system.

I am not going to worry about the empty Yankee Stadium because there are so many minor league games to attend and travel to. However, it has become apparent to Jim and me that we have become more interested in seeing many of the obscure parts of the United States than merely watching baseball games. As a resident of Manhattan, the larger cities where the Triple-A teams reside, such as Buffalo, Syracuse, Richmond, Charlotte, Indianapolis, Peoria, and Harrisburg, do not intrigue me. The readers must wonder why I did not visit some of the interesting ballparks within reach of the greater New York City Metropolitan Area. To me, it did not seem adventurous enough, as I drove by these various parks many times in my youth and was somewhat familiar with the respective areas.

Wanting to see the country towns and meet the people, I was reminded of what my mother used to say about vacationers: "If you live by the sea, take vacations in the mountains. If you live in a mountainous region, vacation at the ocean." At the Triple-A level, however, fans get to watch players teetering on the verge of the majors, in addition to the dubious talents that have been sent back down from the major leagues. One would think that all the top college players would start right in Triple-A, but they are sprinkled throughout the Class A minor league levels at the outset. Remember that the aluminum bats used in college are a negative, as players must get accustomed to the wooden bats in the minor leagues—and, of course, when they make it to *THE SHOW.*

Utica

In August 1995, Jim and I drove to Utica, New York, which is approximately 90 miles northwest of Albany, or 239 miles from New York City. It is located on the Mohawk River, at the foot of the Adirondack Mountains, population sixty-two thousand. Formerly, it was a river settlement of the Mohawk tribe of the Iroquois. Like other Rust Belt cities, Utica had an economic downturn in mid-twentieth century, much of it due to the closure of textile mills and furniture factories.

The Griffiss Air Force Base, located in Rome, New York, about fifteen miles northwest of Utica, was part of the post–Cold War drawdown in 1995. The base closure meant that five thousand jobs, or 30 percent of the city's economic base, was lost. Jim and I took a tour of the Matt Brewery, producer of Saranac beer. Well, we had a few brews, the last one named Billy Beer. It is the fourth-oldest family-owned brewery in America. Founded in 1888 by Francis Xavier Matt, who worked in a brewery in Baden, Germany but immigrated to America in 1880, it originally was called The West End Brewing Co. In the 1980s, Matt's son had a poetic flare, which he used in the Brewery's marketing, and it was posted in the Beer Hall:

Look out Bud! Look out Miller

New Matt's Light is a giant killer
With taste that's great and body surprising
Look out you guys—a new sun is arising

We're not very big compared to you
But we love our beer and know how to brew—
A great light beer—with malt and hops
Shove over guys—your monopoly stops

We went to the Utica ballpark to see the Utica Blue Sox, affiliated with the Boston Red Sox, play the Elmira Pioneers. Utica's baseball cap was the best, with two small blue socks on the front. I don't buy the hat or T-shirt at most games, but this cap I had to have. The Blue Sox jumped off to a 3–0 lead in the first inning when number 14, Jim Chamblee, hit a towering three-run shot to dead center, over 420 feet from home plate. In the program, he was listed as six foot three, 190 pounds, age twenty-one, from Denton, Texas. He last played at Odessa Junior College. The catcher for Utica was Virgil Chevalier, six foot two, 225 pounds, age twenty-one, from Kenosha, Wisconsin. He last played for Seminole Junior College. He hit a home run in the eighth inning that is still going today. Utica beat Elmira 5 to 1.

Besides the caps, the minor leagues feature many unique names, such as the Albuquerque Isotopes, Akron Rubber Ducks, Batavia Muckdogs, Biloxi Shuckers, Rancho Cucamonga Quakes, Lansing Lugnuts, Pensacola Blue Wahoos, Sacramento River Rats, Toledo Mudhens, and Savannah Bananas.

The next day, we drove west to Clinton, New York, to see Hamilton College, about 8 miles southwest of Utica. We took a tour around the campus, which sits on a hilltop overlooking a New England style village of Clinton. The college was named after Alexander Hamilton, the first Secretary of the US Treasury. It is a private liberal arts institution of about 1,800 students, chartered in 1812.

Finger Lakes

We then headed west toward the Finger Lakes, which are southwest of Syracuse, pulling into Skaneateles, which sits at the very top of Lake Skaneateles, an Iroquois term for "long lake." There was a boatyard in town noted for the building of Lightning sailboats. We drove down and back both sides of this picturesque body of water. We had lunch in the town and reminisced about our days of sailing in Lightning boats at the Riverside Yacht Club in Riverside, Connecticut, on Long Island Sound.

Larchmont

The Larchmont Yacht Club Race Week was a very competitive week for racing Lightnings, a nineteen-foot centerboard sloop. Back around 1957, Alex Platt and I were crewing for Kent Bloomer in his Saybrook Lightning. There were about thirty-five boats in the final race on Saturday, which had us tacking over to the north shore of Long Island, and then there was a broad reach back home to the finish line.

We were in thirty-first place as we came around the last marker. Kent said to us, "Should we take a chance and put up the spinnaker?" The wind was not completely behind our backs but partially across as in a broad reach, so we decided to pull the jib down and put the spinnaker up, which was a bit risky as the wind was blowing at about twenty knots. Kent let the mainsail out as far as it would go, and all three of us sat together in the stern so we would not go under bow first. Well, we raced by five boats within seconds as if they were standing still. Kent was beaming with pride with his decision. Suddenly, the stern started to rise as the nose of the boat went under the water. This is what they call "pitchpoling," which is capsizing end over end. The next thing we knew, we were all swimming in Long Island Sound, and within fifteen minutes, the Coast Guard boat was rescuing us and our boat. Kent lost several items on the boat, including two wooden paddles, a stopwatch, and some cushions. We were towed back into the Larchmont Yacht Club harbor, and our dates for the night were all dressed up waiting for us at the dock. Needless to say, we were not the most attractive-looking young eighteen-year-olds about to attend the Race Week Saturday dance.

Caprice was the name of Kent's boat, so I looked in a *Webster Dictionary* the next day back in Riverside and found the following: (1) a sudden unpredictable turn or change, (2) an impulsive, causeless change of mind.

The next evening, Kent met with his father and was expecting angry comments. On the contrary, he congratulated Kent for taking a chance when way behind in the race.

Newark, New York

Our next destination was forty miles to Newark. For a few miles, we drove alongside of the Erie Canal, which we read later was completed in 1825 after starting construction in 1817. The water in the canal was up high and quite beautiful as motorboats were going along at a pretty good clip. The canal ran 363 miles from Albany on the Hudson River to Buffalo. It was very beneficial to the New York business world. We had some time to kill before the game in Newark, so we drove due north to Sodus Point, which is a small village North East of Rochester, a community surrounded on three sides by Lake Ontario. We dipped our toes in the cold water just to say we had been there.

We drove back to Newark to see the Barge Bandits play the Jamestown Jammers. These teams play in the North Atlantic Baseball League, an Independent league that started in 1995 and had already seen five of their original players sign with major league organizations.

We arrived early for the game. Adult general admission was four dollars. Seating capacity was two thousand, and both foul lines were 329 feet. I noticed that all three umpires were standing around home plate before the teams came out to practice, so I walked out on the field and over to home plate to introduce myself, asking them, "Who is the best player on the field today so I can focus in on him?"

The head ump said without hesitation, "The pitcher for the Barge Bandits is really good."

"Tell me about him."

"Well, he has an assortment of pitches that most batters cannot touch. His fastball is easy cheese, he has a wicked slider, and he even throws an occasional knuckle. But you won't believe this: the scouts will not bother to come see him play."

"Why?" I asked.

"Because he is only five foot nine and his heater is not in the mid-90s."

An hour or so later, we sat down to watch this "midget" pitch. He had a one-hitter going into the eighth-inning, and his manager pulled him—I assumed to save his arm. We departed the ballpark with the Bandits leading by 6 to 0.

Elmira

The next morning, we drove seventy-five miles south to Elmira, stopping off at Hobart and William Smith colleges in Geneva, located at the top of Seneca Lake, one of the Finger Lakes. We drove around the campus for about an hour. It was founded in 1822, a small liberal arts college of 2,351 students, 53 percent male, 47 percent female, and 20 percent minority, including international students. Among the student body, 67 percent were from New York and New England. Tuition was $49,677, while room and board was $12,583. The endowment in 2014 was $202 million. It was a very attractive campus on the edge of Lake Seneca.

Drove down Route 14, the western side of Lake Seneca, one of the Finger Lakes, which is a group of eleven long, narrow, roughly north-south lakes in Central New York. Shapes of the lakes are reminded early mapmakers of human fingers, and the name stuck. Seneca is 618 feet deep and is among the deepest in the United States. It is sometimes called the "thumb." The Finger Lakes area is New York's largest wine-producing area.

We arrived in Elmira that afternoon in time to see the Elmira Pioneers play the Albany Diamond Dogs. The Pioneers are a Class A team affiliated with Florida Marlins. Elmira is one of only five cities that have had minor league ball for more than a century, and more than four hundred major leaguers have played there. The town is now on its third stadium in 106 years. Dunn Field, a three-year-old-park, has one of baseball's more bizarre claims to fame. It was there, forty-three years ago, that Don Zimmer was married at home plate. He was a journeyman infielder for twelve years who came up with the Brooklyn Dodgers in 1954. He was part of the original 1962 Mets, who lost a record 120 games. He gained a reputation as one of the best third-base coaches ever, a field position that is arguably second in importance only to that of the manager himself. He was a coach for several teams, including Tampa Devil Rays, where Joe Maddon, now World Series champion Cubs manager in 2016, said that Zimmer was probably the best strategist he had ever been associated with. Maddon credited him specifically for convincing him to use the first-and-third safety squeeze play. His nicknames were Zim and Popeye. He last served as bench coach to Joe Torre during the Yankees last dynasty, from 1996 to 2003. Joe was fond of saying baseball is a game that you have to prove yourself to yourself every day.

Famous players who played at Dunn Field and later made it to the show include Babe Ruth, Wade Boggs, and Curt Schilling, Johnny Mize, and Eddie Murray. We met the team's general manager, Clyde Small, who was asked about their mascot. "We hung ours in effigy a couple of years ago. He was not too exciting, and we decided to get rid of him." Elmira and Utica were members of the New York-Penn Class A league, known as the Pony League.

The announcer on the public address system was a bit of a character throughout the game. After one of the Albany Diamond Dog players struck out, the announcer said, "Sit down in your seat." Later on, he came up with a difficult trivial pursuit question: Before the DH, what pitcher hit two grand slams in one game? Answer: Tony Cloninger.

The game went into the eleventh inning tied 1 to 1. I'm not sure why it was such a low-scoring game. Either neither team could hit or the pitching was really good. Anyway, Elmira got a base runner to third with two outs. As a southpaw, the pitcher would automatically have his back to the runner on third base as he came to his stretch. This would give the runner room to wander off the bag toward home plate. With the count at three balls and one strike, the pitcher probably forgot there was a man on third base. He suddenly went into a full windup, and much to everyone's surprise, the runner took off for home plate and stole home to win the game. The Albany players were stunned. The Elmira players were jumping up and down as they came out of the dugout to swarm the runner.

The program had an article entitled, "Ever Wonder How It Began?"

1. Bullpen: Most parks in the old days sported large billboards advertising "Bull Durham" tobacco. They usually were located in the outfield corners where relief pitchers warmed up. Thus, came the term "bullpen," first used back in 1888. 2. FAN: When Chris Von de Ahe,

genial German owner of the St. Louis team in the 1880's, a noted fan who seldom missed a game, he commented: "Dot feller's a regular FAN-a-tic with the accent on the first syllable."

We were told the population of Elmira was about twenty-nine thousand down from a peak of fifty thousand in 1950. In 1849, the New York and Erie Railroad was built through Elmira, giving the area a New York City to Buffalo route. In 1864, there were 12,123 Confederate soldiers incarcerated in Elmira. The inmates dubbed the camp "Hellmira." At the end of the Civil War, each prisoner was given a loyalty oath and a train ticket back home. Recession in the early 1970s and the flood of 1972 destroyed many of the businesses and single-family houses. Today, the primary manufacturing employers are makers of glass, rail products, precise turning machines, fire hydrants, kingpins, and shackles.

Mark Twain (Samuel Clemens)

He spent more than twenty summers in Elmira with his family at his sister-in-law's house. Twain was very interested in organized baseball and became a real baseball fan. He made a point of learning all the rules. His enthusiasm for the game continued near his house outside of Hartford, Connecticut in May 1875, he attended a game with his close friend Reverend Joseph Twichell, to watch a local team, the Hartford Dark Blues, play the Boston Red Stockings. The two teams were organized right after the Civil War. Back in Elmira, he consented to be one of the umpires. Permission was granted to the players to carry umbrellas onto the field for protection from the sun. Players would not be allowed to carry flowers while running the bases. The reserved seats in the lower part of the grandstand were 25 cents, 10 cents in the upper seats.

Mark Twain's next novel was published in 1889: *A Connecticut Yankee in King Arthur's Court*. He wrote in one chapter a segment on the game of baseball, which included the dangers of umpiring. No umpire ever seemed to survive a game without an injury, and as a result, umpiring became unpopular. *San Francisco Chronical*, July 4, 1887, wrote the following article about Samuel Clemens and baseball in Elmira:

Being asked some points about old-fashioned baseball the humorist did not betray his lack of knowledge of the rules, but said: "I'd like to play a game or two of billiards." He did describe himself as a billiard addict. To get relief from continuous hours and days of writing his latest book, Twain would play billiards for 10-12 straight hours. He considered billiards his most productive form of exercise. In 1906, he wrote: "the billiard table is better than the Doctors. It is driving out the heartburn in a most promising way. I have a billiard table on the premises, and I walk not less than ten miles every day with the cue in hand. The games begin right after luncheon, daily and continue until midnight, with two hours intermission for dinner and music. And so, it is nine hours' exercise per day, and ten or twelve for Sunday.

Twain understood the excessive heat under an umbrella or in the judges' stand about a hundred feet from the home plate. The old-fashioned "wet or dry" method of choosing the first innings was observed, and the marks of spit on a flat stone decided that "the Alerts should go to the bat. Five innings were played." This certainly was a very old-fashined way to get the game started.

Mark Twain was born in Florida, Missouri, which today is uninhabited. His family moved four years later to Hannibal, Missouri. He died in 1910 in Redding, Connecticut, and the body was transported on a train from Redding to Grand Central Station, then to Brick Church on Fifth Avenue for his funeral, after which he was taken to Hoboken and trained to Elmira, where he was put to his final rest. His entire family is buried in Elmira.

In the morning, we drove south along the Chemung River, eventually making our way along the Susquehanna River on Route 6, which was following the river like a snake. Made our way through Scranton, then south to Easton, Pennsylvania, the home of Dixie Cup, Ingersoll Rand, and Lafayette College, and the birthplace of Jimmy and Billy Bourne. Once we crossed the Delaware River, heading east, we were only an hour and a half from New York City.

CHAPTER 4

SEATTLE, TACOMA, YAKIMA, EVERETT, AND CHICAGO

The Beauty of the Northwest

Our next trip, July 28 to August 3, 1999, started in Seattle, Washington. The state of Washington is the only state named for a president. It is the twentieth largest state in size. Olympia is the capital of the state. As most tourists do, we visited the Pike Street Market in downtown Seattle, where locals buy fresh fish and the workers toss 10-pound salmon to each other across the room. Everyone cheers, and then they wrap it up and give it to the customer.

After a delicious lunch at Cutter's restaurant of chowder with lobster and king salmon, we drove to Bainbridge Island to visit with John and Lyn Sinclair. I grew up in Riverside, Connecticut, in the early 1940s about one-eighth of a mile from John. Our two families lived near the Riverside Yacht Club, where we were avid sailors or tennis players. Bainbridge is a wooded island with a population of 17,500 in an area the size of Manhattan. It is an easy ferryboat commute to Seattle.

We then visited with Tim Burns in the eastern section of Seattle, near Madison Park. Tim was the former headmaster of St. David's School at Eighty-Ninth Street and Madison Ave., one block from my home in New York City. He was the head of school during my son Michael's seventh and eighth grades. His new job was headmaster of the Bush School, a private school also in eastern Seattle.

Yakima

Early the next morning we drove about 140 miles southeast to Yakima. We stopped off on the way to drive up Mount Rainier, the highest point in state of Washington, with an elevation of 14,410 feet. It is considered an active volcano even though it has not erupted since 1894. It was named in 1792 by the English Explorer George Vancouver after a fellow navigator Admiral Peter Rainier. The native American name for the mountain, Tahoma, means "The mountain that was God." It does have active steam vents and periodic earth tremors.

We arrived in Yakima that afternoon, mostly flat terrain with rolling prairies. It is one of the most ideal spots in the world to grow cherries and peaches. The town was very clean, and the dominant industry was fruit.

Our box seats were near first base in the sixth row for $6.50 per ticket. We saw the Yakima Bears lose 7 to 5 to the Southern Oregon Timberjacks. The Bears' shortstop and second baseman always covered second base with a runner on third every time the catcher threw the ball back to the pitcher. Certainly, there was no confidence in the catcher's ability to throw the ball accurately back to the pitcher. I had not seen that done since the days of my grammar school team. During the seventh inning break, Frisbees were tossed around the stands. I caught one and tossed it farther up in the stands. The guy next to me told me that the Frisbee represented a free pizza. Oh well! On the second page in the program, in big caps, it read "Free car wash to the dirtiest car in the parking lot."

Mount St. Helens

The next morning, we headed west to Tacoma, stopping to tour, as much of Mount St. Helens as we were permitted. It is located about 50 miles northeast of Portland, Oregon. The eruption happened Sunday, May 18, 1980. It was the single-most powerful natural disaster in American history. Some five thousand miles of logging roads surrounded the volcano. Had it blown just twenty-four hours later, hundreds of loggers working in the region's old-growth forests would have perished. The elevation was 9,677 feet before the eruptions began, and it went to 8,364 feet. We saw some pre-eruption pictures: Helens was a beautiful, symmetrical cone of dazzling white, which was hard for us to imagine when we saw thousands of trees on the ground, which looked like tooth picks strewn as far as the eye could see. It was an awesome sight. There were 230 miles of timber after the eruption. It devastated 200 square miles.

Another picture we were shown was of Spirit Lake, which was magnificent water at the foot of the north face of the mountain. It had since been obliterated by the volcano. The north flank of the mountain had collapsed. In Steve Olson's book *Eruption*, he wrote,

> A striking feature of the event was its silence. Those near the volcano did not hear it. Like the ash cloud—which rose to a height of 60,000 feet—the sound waves traveled upward rather than outward: they were also muffled by great plumes of ash. People as far away as Edmonton, Alberta, and Butte, Montana heard a sonic boom, but those in the volcano's shadow heard only the unnerving sound of trees thudding to the ground." The mountain was named after Baron St. Helens who was at the time the British Ambassador to Spain. Some Indians of the Pacific Northwest called Mount St. Helens "Louwala-Clough," or "smoking mountain.

Late that day, we drove to Tacoma to see Rick Fisher's brother, Bert. He took us for a swim in Lakewood, Washington in Gravelly Lake, called Cook-al-chy (meaning pond Lily) by the native people. That evening, we drove to Cheney Stadium, built in 1960, to watch the Tacoma Rainiers play. It was a clear evening, which enabled us to see Mount Rainier. Juan Marichal was a pitcher for Tacoma many years ago and became a member of the Hall of Fame while playing for the San Francisco Giants.

Everett

The next day we drove north on Route 5 for an hour to Everett to see the Everett Aqua Sox play the Boise Hawks. Mario Mendoza was a pitcher for Boise and later was pitching well for the New York Yankees. Everett and Boise were in the Northwest Class A league. It is a short season of a seventy-six-game schedule, starting the third week of June and closing the second week of September. The league is composed of eight teams, from Idaho to Portland to Spokane to Everett. Professional baseball returned in 1984, when Bob and Margaret Bavasi purchased the Walla Walla Blue Mountain Bears and moved the Northwest League franchise to Everett. The club quickly gained a reputation for its clean ballpark, wacky promotions, and fan friendliness. The sun was very bright at game time, 6:05

p.m. the right fielder missed a pop fly hit right near him because he just could not see it in the sun. In between first and second inning, the vendors were throwing hot dogs, rolled up in tin foil, from top of the dugouts to the fans.

There was constant entertainment on the field in between innings, including a small pig running all over the field. The view from our seven-dollar seats of the snow-capped Cascade Mountains in the distance was breathtaking. For dinner, my brother and I had clam chowder in a bowl of bread, a salmon sandwich, and a local beer, brewed by The Flying Pig Brewing Co. Here I was, with my brother watching my favorite sport, eating fresh fish and gazing upon beautiful scenery in the background. We looked at each other and said, "It just doesn't get any better than this."

In the middle of the game, we met the president of the Everett Aquasox, Mark Sperandio. He was very curious about the two guys who had flown from the East Coast to Seattle to watch minor league baseball games.

There was a unique advertisement in the program, entitled, "Read Your Way to A Free AquaSox Ticket." It read,

> What is easy to use, free, educational, provides hours of fun for children during summer vacation, and can earn you and your child a free AquaSox ticket? Children who participate in the 1999 Summer Reading Adventure record their completed books or time spent reading. When they are halfway to their goal, they receive a ticket good for two to the August 1 or August 17 AquaSox game. Children who reach their summer reading goal earn a free paperback book.

This was sponsored by several local companies, including Boeing Employees' Credit Union, US Bank, Washington Mutual, Elder Corp, and Everett Mutual Bank.

Seattle Mariners

We decided to make a few exceptions to our minor league trips by attending some major league games. The first one was back in Seattle to see the Seattle Mariners play in their brand-new Safeco Field. This unique stadium was built by Safeco Property and Casualty Insurance Co., which was founded in Seattle in 1923. The Mariners played its first thirty-nine games in 1999 in the Kingdome before opening Safeco Field for its final forty-two home contests. The Mariners beat the Baltimore Orioles 3 to 1, even though Mike Mussina pitched five shut-out innings for Baltimore. Ken Griffey Jr., outfielder for Seattle, missed two fly balls in the sun that dropped right near him. Luckily, the Mariners won despite these two unusual plays.

Our seats were at the field level for twenty-five dollars per person on a bright, sunny afternoon, and of course, the retractable roof was open. Around the end of the fifth inning, there was a freight train that was traveling behind the center-field fence, blowing its whistle. It was something one would expect more in a minor league park. In the program, it described the roof as an Engineering Marvel. The span is 655 feet or nearly two football fields. On calm days, the panels can close into position in 8.5 minutes. In conditions with wind speeds of no more than thirty miles per hour, the roof will change positions in twenty minutes. If wind speeds exceed thirty miles per hour, the roof will not be moved.

Sammy Sossa

The second exception of seeing only minor league games was during our flight back east, when we stopped off in Chicago to see Sammy Sosa play for the Chicago Cubs at Wrigley Field. We checked into the Drake Hotel, went right to the ballpark, and were in our seats by the first inning, when Sammy *went yard* over the famous ivy-covered left field wall. What a treat that was for us! Sosa was from the Dominican Republic and became a member of the Chicago Cubs in 1992, where he became renowned as one of the game's best hitters. He was the National League home-run leader in 2000 and 2002, was voted an All-Star seven times and National League MVP in 1998. Sam is also the only player to have hit sixty or more homers in a single season three times.

Wrigley Field, originally known as Weeghman Field, was built on the North Side of Chicago in 1915 at a cost of $215,000. Charles Weeghman, a successful restaurant owner, sold part of the Chicago Cubs to J. Ogden Armour and William Wrigley. By 1918, Wrigley owned most of the Chicago Cubs.

From the beginning, there were small houses looking into right and left field. The rooftops were lined with folding chairs for viewing the game. These were later converted to bleachers as the team bought most of these houses beginning in 2002. Wrigley Field became the official name in 1926. Bill Veeck Jr., working with Wrigley, installed ivy on all the outfield walls in 1937. Sometimes, fly balls landed in the ivy and were ruled a double. The reaction of the new ivy was mixed at first but soon became part of this unique ballpark. The Ricketts family bought the Chicago Cubs in 2009. Wrigley Field is the second oldest baseball stadium in America, as Fenway Park, in Boston, is number one.

CHAPTER 5
ILLINOIS, IOWA, AND HANNIBAL, MISSOURI

The Fascinating Life of Samuel Clemens

August 2000, we traveled to Illinois, Iowa, and Missouri. We drove from Chicago's O'Hare Airport west to Nachusa Conservancy, then to Galena in the extreme northwest corner of the state. In 2018, I did some research on Nachusa and discovered that the local people had done an amazing job of purchasing remnant pieces of prairie and cornfields, for a total of 397 acres. In the early 1800s, Illinois was covered in 22 million acres of prairie. Today, only 0.1 percent remains of the entire ecosystem. The killing of bison, for sport and to make way for the American cattle industry, reduced the total number of bison to about a thousand in 1894. The Conservancy today has 3,500 acres of tallgrass prairie, with one hundred bison roaming freely.

Ulysses S. Grant

On our way to Galena, we saw nothing but cornfields and peas. We took a tour of Ulysses S. Grant's house, a simple brick house with four bedrooms and original furnishings. A group of townspeople presented the house to Grant in 1865 on his victorious return from the Civil War. He had moved to Galena in 1860. He did not live there very long, as he was elected president after the war. His remains were re-interred in a mausoleum on Riverside Drive in New York City.

Grant biography, written by Ron Chernow, was published in 2017, a very thorough and interesting biography of Ulysses S. Grant. His other works include *Washington: A Life* and a renowned biography of Alexander Hamilton, which inspired the Broadway musical.

Grant was born April 27, 1822, in Point Pleasant, Ohio, in a one-room house near the Ohio River, 25 miles east of Cincinnati. As a simple Westerner, he attended and graduated from West Point. He struggled for most of his life with various degrees of alcoholism. He had a distinguished career in the Mexican War. In 1864, he led the Union Forces to defeat the Confederacy. He put into movement the railroads and telegraphs, which helped to coordinate his men in beating the southern forces. President Lincoln respected General Grant and had much confidence in his ability. Grant's soldiers had fewer casualties than the Confederate men.

Grant was the eighteenth president, from 1869 to 1877. He was constantly working on gaining freedom and civil rights for the Blacks. He helped create the Fifteenth Amendment to give Blacks the right to vote. He also wanted to eliminate the Ku Klux Klan, an American white supremacist hate group. At its peak in the 1920s, Klan membership exceeded four million people nationwide.

Mark Twain convinced Grant to write his own biography during the last couple of years of his life. He was suffering from throat cancer but worked many hours a day to complete the book. It was completed on July 16, 1885, one week before his death.

Clinton

We then drove 50 miles south along the Mississippi River on the Illinois side, crossed over the river at Savanna to the Iowa side, and eventually made our way to Clinton, Iowa.

At the height of its local economy during the late nineteenth century, Clinton was regarded as the lumber capital of the nation. Today, agriculture plays a big part in Clinton's economy, which is visible in the beautiful rolling fields filled with luscious, fresh harvest crops.

We then went straight to Riverview Stadium, which was built on the western banks of the Mississippi River. We saw the Clinton Lumber Kings beat the Lansing Lug Nuts 7–0 in the Midwest Class A League. By the seventh inning, my brother and I realized that the Clinton pitcher, six-foot-three, 185-pound Scott Dunn, had not only a no-hitter going but also a perfect game. Clinton scored four runs in the bottom of the seventh inning when I told Jim that this could tighten up the pitcher's arm as he waited on the bench.

He comes out for the top of the eighth and throws three straight balls to the first batter. Luckily, the batter proceeded to pop up, and the next two batters made outs. Top of the ninth, all the fans stood up cheering for the pitcher, who proceeded to strike out the side. All his teammates mobbed the pitcher, pouring a keg of beer over his head. It was the only perfect game in the history of the Lumber Kings. Last perfect game in the Midwest League was in 1975. Dunn, who struck out a total of twelve, was selected by the Cincinnati Reds in the tenth round. He played collegiate ball at University of Texas. The next day in the local paper, it stated Dunn had thrown ninety-seven pitches, including seventy-two strikes. He went to a three-ball count only twice. He used a variety of off-speed pitches to complement his fastball, which was clocked at eighty-nine to ninety-one miles per hour most of the night, topping out at ninety-three. For dinner that night at the ballpark: one hot dog and a root beer for two dollars.

Dunn played in the minor leagues before appearing briefly with the Angels in 2004, then reappearing in the major leagues with the Tampa Bay Devil Rays in 2006. He pitched in the Oakland Athletics minor league system in 2007. Following the season, Dunn retired from professional baseball.

Octagonal Barns

The next morning, we continued south along the muddy Miss, then headed west to the town of Downey, just southeast of Iowa City, to see an octagonal-shaped red barn, of which there are several in that part of Iowa. Just south we went through West Liberty, where there was the Strand Theatre on Main Street, which reminded me of Truman Capote's line In Cold Blood: "A movie house stands stark and cheerless on Main Street." This scene was a throwback to the 1920s. It was the real Midwest. To view a few more round barns, we decided to drive to the southern part of Iowa to a verdant old-world highway dotted with picturesque towns, hugged by history book trails, was Route 2, which ran east-west in the southern part of Iowa, only 10 to 15 miles from the Missouri border. We saw magnificent barns, quaint villages, an Amish store, and several historic sites. A typical barn was 60 feet high, 70 feet in diameter, and 220 feet in circumference. In 1986 there were fourteen octagonal barns in the state of Iowa. Most of them were built from 1883 to 1905. One octagonal barn was built in 1905, three miles north of Leon. These seemingly simple structures were presisely crafted to fit the needs of the farmer and the farm. The central floor was open for wheat threshing. European barns style included stables and sleeping quarters. English barns had small stabling areas for the family horse and hay storage. By the mid 1800s, basements were added and were used for manure storage. In the 1900s, concrete flooring became more common especially to replace wood or dirt floors. And it was more sanitary.

A few interesting details about the barns: (1) The cupolas were not just for decoration. The cupola was a way to vent moisture and excess heat and create movement of fresh air in the barn. (2) Barns were usually outfitted with a handful of lightning rods on top of the roof. The cable was attached to another rod, which was placed into the ground. The rods would drain off the excess static in the clouds and release it into the ground.

After leaving Leon, we drove east to Burlington, Iowa, to meet a Notre Dame classmate, Jake Moreland. Jake practiced law in Ottumwa, which is located on the Des Moines River seventy-five miles southeast of Des Moines. On the way to the ballpark, we were behind a pickup truck with a gun rack in the rear window. A ten-year-old boy sat near his dad in the truck. Surprisingly, there was a rear bumper sticker that said: "What part of *f—k you* don't you understand?" How could a family man have that near his license plate?

Burlington

We were next on our way to Burlington, which was explored in 1673 by Marquette and Joliet. The area changed hands from France to Spain, back to France, and finally to the United States as part of the Louisiana Purchase. When Iowa was named a territory in 1868, Burlington remained the capital. Today, the hills, valleys, and prairies and the Mississippi River create the perfect scenic backdrop.

The French explorers believed the Mississippi River emptied into the Sea of Japan. The River's source is Lake Itasca, a glacial lake in northern Minnesota, and unfortunately in the twenty-first century, there is an agriculture runoff from states that surround the Mississippi River, such as Minnesota, Wisconsin, Illinois, Iowa, Missouri, Arkansas, to name just a few. Fertilizer and manure used by the farmers have phosphorus and nitrogen. Chicken production in Arkansas is up over 50 percent in the past two decades. The pollution from chicken farms and slaughterhouses seep into the Arkansas River, which in turn dumps into the Mississippi. Nitrates in Kansas have tainted wells near the Missouri River, which then pollutes the Mississippi.

Runoff happens when water from rainfall or melting snow picks up the excess nutrients along with other sediment as it moves toward bodies of water. Intensive farming practices strip nutrients from the soil. As a result, farmers have to add fertilizer to the soil to replace the nutrients. Under fertilization causes lower yields and poor-quality produce farmers tend to error on the side of caution and over-fertilize their crops. The five most polluted waterways in the United States: the Ohio River, Mississippi River, Tennessee River, Houston Ship Channel, and Pacific Ocean. The Mississippi flows 2,320 miles to the Gulf of Mexico.

Mississippi means "large river" to the Chippewa Indians. It is still second in length to the Missouri River. It is joined by the Ohio River to form the lower Mississippi River. It runs through ten states, and numerous towns have French names, such as Prairie duChien, LaCrosse, Fond du lac, and Frontenac in Wisconsin. There are LaCrescent and LaMoille in Minnesota; Prairie du Rocher in Illinois; DesMoines, Dubuque, and Marquette in Iowa; Refuge in Arkansas; Cape Girardeau, Cahokia, and Portage des Sioux in Missouri; French Camp, Fayette, and Beauregard in Mississippi; and Baton Rouge, Lafayette, and New Orleans in Louisiana.

The river system in America was comprised of the Mississippi, Ohio and Missouri rivers, which carried most of the immigrants and freight that settled the Midwest.

The Burlington Bees beat the Beloit Snappers 9 to 3. Two relatives of Spencer Oborn (well, sort of relatives) hit a home run for the Bees, and Matt Borne was their pitcher. Community Field, first built in 1947, was a small ballpark with a seating capacity of 3,200. All the seats were opposite the infield.

In the program, it stated that some weekday games began at 11:30 a.m. because the Burlington Bees specified several games early in the season as "Honor Roll and Reading Club Days," inviting local school kids to Community Field to celebrate their successes in the classroom.

In one of the late innings, the song, "I got stung," an Elvis classic, was blasted on the public address system. The fans participated and really loved it. The Bees had several players who made it to the big leagues, such as Billy Williams, Sal Bando, Paul Molitor, and Vida Blue. Molitor, Williams, and Blue had their uniform numbers retired. I purchased a Bees cap for my friend back home, Gary Shilling, who is a beekeeper.

Mark Twain

Heading south the next morning to St. Louis, I was looking over the *Rand McNally Road Atlas* as we entered Missouri from Keokuk, Iowa, along the Mississippi. I learned from previous trips that there is a fountain of information on Rand McNally maps printed in red or blue. On this trip, I saw the town of Hannibal, Missouri, and printed just underneath in red: Mark Twain's Boyhood Home and Museum. So, we drove right down to the edge of the Mississippi into the old part of Hannibal. Looking around for a place to have our breakfast, we saw Becky Thatcher's Diner. What better place to eat than in Tom Sawyer's girlfriend's restaurant!

As was our custom, Jim and I sit at the counter, preferably where we both have people sitting next to us. I said good morning to the man next to me but got only a grumble back from him. My next trick to get people to talk was to bring out the map of Missouri, open it up, and ask Jim, in a somewhat loud voice, "What do you think is the best route to St. Louis?" Both men on either side of us put their newspapers down and began to answer the question. Well, the man next to me, believe it or not, was the retired headmaster of the local grammar school. I immediately asked him how often the students read Mark Twain books. He said that all the kids were required to read Mark Twain books in most of the grades. He was a most interesting man to converse with. Each year, at least two or three plays based on Samuel Clemens's books were performed by the students.

My curiosity of Mark Twain was tweaked enough to read a biography written by Ron Powers in 2004. Powers did an immense amount of research as he wrote the book in chronological order and would insert passages from Twain's notebooks, letters, books—627 pages in all.

Living in Hannibal from ages seven to seventeen, it became obvious that there was one important influence in Mark Twain's thinking: the Mississippi River, which helped to develop his dreams, imagination, and fantasies. These characteristics expanded when he wrote *Life on the Mississippi River* (1883), *The Adventures of Tom Sawyer* (1876), and *The Adventures of Huckleberry Finn* (1884). In these books, he displayed his genius for dialect and creating unusual characters. And to think that he wrote these three books with just a grammar-school education. Twain himself became a voracious reader, which led him to writing very erudite sentences of the dialogue with interesting descriptions of specific scenes, such as the graveyard locale in *Adventures of Tom Sawyer*.

Here are several paragraphs from that scene:

> Tom lay awake and waited. The howl of a far-off dog rose on the night air, and was answered by a fainter howl. And now the tiresome chirping of a cricket … the clock chimed eleven. And then there came, a most melancholy caterwauling. A single minute later he was dressed and out the window and creeping along the roof of the ell on all fours. … Huckleberry Finn, with his dead cat, was wading with Tom through the tall grass of the graveyard. It was a graveyard of the old fashioned Western kind. It had a crazy board fence around it, which leaned inward in places, and outward the rest of the time, but stood upright nowhere.

> All the old graves were sunken in, there was not a tombstone on the place. A faint wind moaned through the trees, and Tom feared it might be the spirits of the dead. The hooting of a distant owl was all the sound that traveled the dead stillness. Tom said in a whisper:

Do you believe the dead people like it for us to be here? Huckleberry whispered: I wish I knowed. It's awful solemn like, ain't it?

Presently, Tom seized his comrade's arm and said Sh! What'll we do? I donno. Think they will see us? Oh, Tom, they can see in the dark, same as cats. I wisht I hadn't come. Oh, don't be afeared I'll try to, Tom but Lord, I'm all of a shiver.

Some vague figures approached through the gloom, swinging an old-fashioned tin lantern that freckled the ground with innumerable little spangles of light. It's the devils, sure enough. Three of 'em. Lordy, Tom, we're gonners. Can you pray?"[1]

As his house was only one block from the River, it was convenient and easy to sneak out at night to meet his three buddies down by the River's edge. Just think of how quiet it was around midnight, accompanied by various noises from different four-legged animals, not to mention the screeching sounds of foxes, the eerie calls of Common Loons plus bullfrogs. At ages 13–14, this took a while getting used to. And of course, they had to "borrow" two skiffs to row to the other side of the River or to one of the islands where they pretended to be pirates, plus picked pecans and razzberries. They would even venture across when the River was frozen. In the middle of the River, they would hear all of the animal sounds at the same time which would add to their timid and apprehensive feelings. In short, they were down-right scared. But later-on they enacted "the art of Pirating" along the river's edge.

In the preface of the *Tom Sawyer* book, Twain says, "Most of the adventures recorded in this book really occurred; one or two were experiences of my own, the rest of those boys who were school classmates of mine. Huck Finn is drawn from life; Tom Sawyer also, but not from an individual---he is a combination of the characteristics of three boys whom I knew." Geoffrey Sanborn wrote in the afterword, "The book was strictly a history of a boy."[2]

---

[1] Mark Twain, *The Adventures of Tom Sawyer.*
[2] Twain, *The Adventures of Tom Sawyer.*

The Sam Clemens's family ran into hard economic times, and Samuel was forced to find work as a typesetter and printer once he completed eighth grade. At age seventeen or eighteen, he decided to visit major cities such as Philadelphia, New York City, Washington, DC, St. Louis, New Orleans, San Francisco, and Virginia City, and he became a roaming reporter for several newspapers. He wrote extensively in his notebooks about the visits to these various cities. He was quoted as saying, "Make your mark in New York, and you are a made man." In 1855 at the age of twenty-one, Sam Clemens was offered a job by his brother Orion for five dollars a week, in his print shop.

Most importantly, this move to Keokuk, Iowa, renewed Sam's boyhood dream to become a pilot on a Mississippi steamboat. He first spent two years as an apprentice steersman when he studied every detail of the River from Hannibal, Missouri, to New Orleans. He then became a full fledge pilot for two years, and those memories produced the book *Life on the Mississippi*. He wrote,

> It is good for steamboating, and good to drink, but it is worthless for all other purposes, except baptizing. There was a nutritiousness in the mud, and a man that drunk Mississippi water could grow corn in his stomach if he wanted to. You look at the graveyards; that tells the tale.

> Trees won't grow worth shucks in a Cincinnati graveyard, but in a St. Louis graveyard they grow upwards of eight hundred foot high. It's all on account of the water the people drunk before they laid up. A Cincinnati corpse don't richen a soil any.

Mark Twain (his nom de plume) was a Mississippi River term meaning "number two." The second mark on the boat line measured depth, signified two fathoms or twelve feet—a safe depth for the steamboat. Hence, Mark (measure) Twain (two).

A legend in his own time, he was known for his clever puns. Here are a few of my favorites:

- "The secret of getting ahead is getting started."
- "You can't depend on your eyes when your imagination is out of focus."

- "Good friends, good books, and a sleepy conscience: this is the ideal life."
- "When I was a boy of fourteen, my father was so ignorant I could hardly stand to have the old man around. But when I got to be twenty-one, I was astonished at how much he had learned in seven years."

In 1861, he started his lecture tours, which took him all over the country. Traveling on trains, he would give lectures in fifty cities within fifty days. His first lecture was in Cleveland, and the last one was in 1869, in Iowa City. These years were somewhat stressful but at the same time were happy and peaceful for Mark Twain. However, his subsequent lectures of the spoken word led him to the world of the written word. But Twain had many interests, which led him to consider being a playwright. As a young adult, he thought seriously of becoming a minister, but in later life, he appeared to have a strained relationship with God, which put him somewhere between an agnostic and an atheist.

On February 2, 1870, Samuel Clemens married Olivia Langdon of Elmira, New York. They courted for some seventeen months, much of it via 189 love letters while Mark was on his lecture tours.

In 1902, Mark Twain returned to Hannibal after several years away, and the girls of the town dressed as Becky Thatcher, and the boys dressed as Tom Sawyer. The museum in town dedicated to Mark Twain had more than a dozen original Norman Rockwell paintings representing Huck Finn and Tom Sawyer. One of his famous quotes: "The lack of money is the root of all evil." He was constantly borrowing money, investing in private deals that were not successful and would put him deeper in debt. In the 1890s, he went on a yearlong lecture tour to avoid bankruptcy. All in all, his accomplishments were many: he produced twenty-eight novels, numerous short stories, several hundred letters, a handful of plays, and many sketches. He received honorary degrees from Cambridge, Oxford, Yale University, and the University of Missouri. He had a way with words.

Another interesting connection to Hannibal, Missouri, was Joe Hardy, born in Hannibal, and played outfield for the baseball Washington Senators in 1956. He was promoted from the minor leagues in midseason and became an instant star at age twenty-two, with a high batting average, twenty-seven home runs, and lots of Runs Batted In.

This perennial last-place team was competing with the New York Yankees for the top of the American League. Both teams faced each other at Griffith Stadium on the last day of the season to determine the champion. The Yankees sent Bob Cerv to the plate as a pinch hitter in the ninth inning, with two men on base and the Senators ahead by one run. A long fly ball was hit into deep left center, with Joe Hardy racing after it. He makes a dramatic catch, never skipping a stride as he ran through an opening in the wall, continuing at full speed and eventually exiting the stadium.

He informed the Senators' management the next day via Western Union telegram that he was retiring from baseball as the team subsequently lost the World Series without Joe Hardy. But his story was told by the stage show on Broadway and followed by the movie *Damn Yankees*. And Joe was known as "Shoeless Joe from Hannibal, Missouri."

Departing from Hannibal, we arrived in St. Louis in time to sit in our seats at Busch Stadium to see the Cardinals beat the Atlanta Braves 9 to 3. Here, I saw one play I had not seen in years, whereby the St. Louis pitcher up at bat hit a hard line drive that one-bounced to the right fielder, who threw the runner out at first base.

Mark McGuire was injured, so we did not get to see him play. He had six seasons of forty or more home runs. He had seventy-two in one season. At least 75 percent of the fans wore some kind of Cardinal red shirt or hat. Very rabid fans!

That evening, we attended a preseason football game in which the St. Louis Rams beat the Oakland Raiders in their new domed stadium. The noise factor was at a high level. Cannot imagine sitting through a season game with the roof closed. The Cardinal and Ram tickets were gifted to us from Joe Dwyer, a native of St. Louis and my roommate during my junior year at Notre Dame.

CHAPTER 6

BILLINGS AND HAVRE, MONTANA, AND CANADA

Grandfather Bourne's Adventure out West

In July 2002, Billings, Montana, was our next baseball destination. It is presently the largest city in the state, with a population of 166,855 in the metropolitan area. Our plane landed on one of the long cliffs, known as Rims, about five hundred feet high overlooking the downtown core of the city.

Founded as a railroad town in 1882, it is located in the south-central portion of the state and borders on the Yellowstone River. The city is named for Frederick H. Billings, a former president of the Northern Pacific Railroad. The other major cities in Montana include Bozeman, Butte, Great Falls, Helena (the capital), and Missoula (University of Montana).

Much of the recent growth of Billings is from the Bakken oil development in eastern Montana and western North Dakota, as well as the Heath shale oil discovery just north of Billings. Granite Peak, elevation of 12,807 feet, in the Beartooth Mountains, is the highest point in the state. It is about 70 miles southeast of Billings. The city received an inch of ash from the eruption of Mount St. Helens in 1980, 850 miles to the west.

Cobb Field is where the Billings Mustangs played the Great Falls Dodgers that evening. Both teams were members of the Pioneer League—Rookie Advanced, founded in 1939. It was comprised of eight teams from Idaho, Montana, Utah, and Alberta (Canada). The Mustangs won that evening in a most uninteresting game except that their relief pitcher in the ninth inning struck out all three batters with a high heater and an unusual slow curve. The fastball must have been close to ninety-five miles per hour, but his curve was no more than seventy-five miles per hour. It reminded me of what Warren Spahn once said: "Hitting is timing. Pitching is upsetting timing."

Miles City*

Many, many homesteaders came to eastern Montana from the midwestern states and several European countries. So we decided to drive about 145 miles east on route 94 to Miles City, and then tour a handful of the smaller towns a little further east. Miles city, population of 8,393 was a renowned "wide open" town that catered to the whims of the cowboy intent on blowing his pay and raising hell. In 1881, the population was 1,000, the town boasted 42 saloons. Dance Halls and brothels lined the streets. Horse races were a popular attraction. The Battle of the Little Bighorn, known as Custer's Last Stand(1876) is two hours due south. Another interesting historical event happened in March 1944. An ice jam on the Yellowstone River caused flooding which reached into Miles City. A B-17 bomber from Rapid City, South Dakota cleared the ice jam using 250 pound bombs. For several years it was the social center of British life in Montana. Northern Pacific Railroad reached Miles City in 1880s. The Cottage Saloon kept a big bowl of Mulligen stew standing on the stove all the time and you could help yourself. If the cowboys wanted to, they could take their blankets and bed down on the floor, and in the morning the saloon owner would give them a free drink.

An Army Camp helped Miles City grow in 1870s followed by a cattle center. Fort Keogh is situated on the south bank of the Yellowstone River, at the mouth of the Tongue River. It was first occupied in 1876 and served as Army infantry and cavalry post until 1900.

Jim and I drove 80 miles east to the little town of Baker, population of 1,910(2018). Some of the best land open to Homestead entry was found near the towns of Baker, Ismay, Marsh, Mildred, Terry. Baker was built along the rail line of the Milwaukee Road. Additional growth came with the discovery of oil and gas in 1912. Terry had a ample underground water supply. Terry became a shipping point for the livestock. It was an important wool producing center, about a million pounds of wool were shipped from the town in 1901. The Union Church was the first permanent house of worship, built in 1906. For a time, services had been held in a wool storage building, and the congregation sat on sacks of wool. The builders added an outhouse in the back. Town of Marsh popped up in 1910 along the railroad tracks. It consisted of a grain elevator, general store, bar and school, all northeast of Terry along the Yellowstone River. The German Lutheran church was opened in 1920. Ministers were forbidden to preach in German. Cowboy shooting was everywhere. One saloon had a sign: Justice of the PIECE.

In this treeless country, the Homesteaders would finance the completion of the railroad network. They came to possess as much land as possible, the big corporations persuaded the railroads to build further west. Schools were built on the prairie every five and six miles. This said that the newcomers were here to stay long term. The train ride was 40 hours from Chicago to Ismay/Baker. Ranchers called Homesteaders: rubes, greenhorns, idiots and Honyockers. Ranchers were hoping that the Homesteaders would fail.

Eastern Montana prairie was one of the most remote and desolate regions of the West. The Badlands of the Yellowstone were full of mule deer, mountain sheep, and grizzly bears. One of the main reasons hunters settled in eastern Montana was the prospect of unlimited hunting in the Outback. They would set up a tent, shack or dig a primitive dugout, for two or three months. After stalking these wild animals, they would usually return home with a winter's supply of meat.

The railroads advertised Montana farmland to the world. Pamphlets were distributed by RR agents all over the United States and Europe. They were translated into German, Swedish, Norwegian, Danish, Russian and Italian. They were spread in barber shops and almost any other retail shops. They were even seen in the New York City EL.

In 1881, the Northern Pacific RR reached Montana, where it hitched itself to the convenient valley of the Yellowstone River. In 1887, the Great Northern arrived; it clung to the Missouri River winding westward to Great Falls. The rush to eastern Montana range reached its peak in 1886. After a warm dry winter and summer drought, by fall the rangelands were nearly bare. An early winter descended in November with a vengeance. Terrible blizzards blanketed the grasses and temperatures plummeted, reaching 60 degrees below zero. Cattle had perished where they lay. The greatest losses occurred in the barren reaches of eastern Montana Territory, where some ranches suffered the loss of 90% of their livestock. In a matter of months many of the corporate ranches had been completely wiped out.

Some cattlemen turned to raising sheep which were cheaper to buy and proved hardier during the deadly winters.

In 1909 the Enlarged Homestead Act increased the size of a Homestead to 320 acres from 160 acres. It just so happened that 1909 fell during a wet cycle. More than 80,000 homesteaders moved into Montana between 1909 and the early 1920s.

One twenty-two year old cowboy for a Texas outfit was given the following instructions by his boss before setting out for Montana with a herd of 2,500 cattle: "tonight, you locate the North Star and you drive straight toward it for three months and you will be in the neighborhood of where I want you to turn loose."

Deer hounds were kept on one ranch on the North Side of the Yellowstone River to protect their herds from wolves and coyotes.

James Hill's Great Northern line had seduced thousands of Homesteaders to Montana. Hill's biographer, Stewart Holbrook, claimed that a children's rhyme made the rounds of Montana school yards along the line of the Great Northern: "Twixt Hell & Hill there's just one letter: Were Hill in Hell we'd feel much better."

A family farm around 1911-12 lost crops valued at $2,000 in a single hailstorm.

Many German-Russian women homesteaded in Eastern Montana. These industrious farm women were supplanting cowgirls as the heroines of the West.

We then drove for a few hours going west and north toward route 94. Ismay was the smallest town in the state with only population of 20, Mildred had 382 people, Terry 561. In summer of 1915 a cyclone ripped through the center of Ismay and turned the town to flying matchwood.

Optimism characterized the early years of Homesteading, especially when rains fell in ample amounts in eastern Montana. After WW1, grain prices collapsed, plagues of locusts descended, and half the farmers in Montana lost their land. Most of the newcomers did not know the state's land and climate. Soils dried up, winds blew the topsoil away. Grasshoppers devoured the crops. And rainy years converted to dry topsoil. About 20,000 mortgages were foreclosed and two million acres went out of cultivation.*

We returned to Billings, and the next morning we planned to drive approximately 247 miles north to Havre, Montana. And of course, we had to find an interesting, unique place for breakfast along the way. Forty miles north on Route 87 is the town of Roundup, population 1,822. Our trip to Roundup provided us with sensational views of the snow-covered Crazy Mountains, elevation of 11,214 feet and 600 square miles. They are almost completely surrounded by private property, which makes it difficult to access. Lots of mountain goats and a few wolverines. No one really knows the truth about how the Crazy Mountains got their name.

One rendition: When the white people came to the region, they asked the natives what they called these mountains. Not understanding each other's languages, they had to communicate in sign language. The natives tried to tell them that the mountains were a place of visions. Imagine the natives waving their hands around, pointing to the sky, wide-eyed, while raising their arms above their heads, over and over. According to David Strong, in his book, *Crazy Mountains*: *Learning from Wilderness to Weigh Technology*, the perplexed whites interpreted these signs to mean a place where people just went crazy. Maybe no one knows the truth. The Crazies made the local people go crazy for decades wondering why?

*four previous pages most were taken from: Photographing Montana 1894-1928 by Donna M. Lucey, The Life of Evelyn Cameron, Alfred A. Knopf 1991.

Roundup

As we are filling up our gas tank at the only gas station in Roundup, a pickup truck pulled in, towing a rig with two horses in the back. A good-looking cowgirl (estimated age of forty), was dressed like a wrangler in denim and dusty leather cowboy boots. She filled the gas tank up and drove seventy-five yards to the only restaurant in town. We proceed to follow a few minutes later, entered the same eatery, and sat down next to her at the counter. Her breakfast arrived: big steak, two eggs on top, hash browns on the side, plus a cup of coffee. We introduced ourselves and discovered she was a horse trainer who was delivering two horses to a client outside Roundup. She lived in Winifred, population 141, about one hundred miles due north, which was in the general direction of Havre. Her ten-year-old son attended a local school of only four other kids. She had to drive thirty-one miles to reach a real supermarket and other stores.

Jawbone Creek Golf Course

Instead of heading north, we decided to get a little venturous and headed west toward the town of Harlowton, which is the county seat of Wheatland County, with a population of 920. On the way we saw a sign: Jawbone Creek Country Club. As golfers, Jim and I said we had to see a golf club with this name. We turned on a dirt road, which took us to the Jawbone golf course and a trailer/mobile home that served as the pro shop. No clubhouse, of course, but we received permission to walk the first hole and followed a twosome who just teed off on the 510-yard par 5 hole. There was a dogleg left halfway to the green, and there were little uniform rows of headstones that sat behind a white picket fence. If you hooked your drive off the first tee, your ball ended in the cemetery. Above the entrance was a sign that read, "Jawbone Cemetery." The club claims that this is the only golf course in America that has a "resting place" inside a golf course. The yardage for the course from the men's tees is 6,593 yards. Ladies' yardage is 5,916.

Harlowton was the end of the line for the railroad. Informally, the local people called the RR "The Jawbone" because there were promising statements made by the line's promoters that contrasted with the company's weak financial position. At one time, years ago, the railroad ran 157-mile stretch between Lewistown and Lombard. The RR was built by Richard Harlow in 1900 to capitalize on the mining of gold, lead, silver, and copper in the area. He sold it to the Chicago, Milwaukee, and St. Paul Railroad, which operated in the area until 1980. Harlow is nestled between three mountain ranges, which helps contribute to mild winters with occasional chinooks and low humidity.

Ferry Boat over Missouri River

Heading farther north, the horse trainer we met in Roundup told us it would be more interesting to float over the Missouri River via the McClelland Ferry than go directly over a bridge. And it is a *free* ride across the Missouri on a flatbed ferry. So, we went one hundred miles north to the Missouri River, with the first forty-five miles in wide-open spaces, not one single town. A great way to see rural America/Montana. Where is everybody?

The first ferry was founded in 1921 by Jack McClelland and his wife. There were two other operating ferries on the Missouri River in Montana. This day, the McClelland Ferry was operated by a woman who used a pulley system to go approximately seventy-five yards in five minutes across the Missouri. A drive cable spanned the river, and a diesel motor powered the ferry. It uses a third of a pint to complete a round trip. She could pull it by hand; it pulls that easy. It would haul forty thousand pounds.

The only other car was a SUV with four guys and their hunting rifles. There were few bighorn sheep in the hills, but these young men were looking for deer. To the north, the town of Chinook was about ninety miles away. Half of those crossing throughout the year are farmers, and the other half are tourists, a portion that's grown significantly. The two surrounding counties cover the cost of operating the ferry. Every season, there are 1,600 to 2,000 crossings. This was so much more interesting than going over a highway bridge that was fourteen miles up the river.

As we crossed the Missouri River on the flatbed ferry, one of the hunters asked me if Jim and I were considering driving east to see the American Prairie Reserve. Having no knowledge of this open land, he explained the details of this unique venture. We chose to continue our journey to Havre, which I realized several years later had been a mistake.

James and Deborah Fallows wrote a book, entitled *Our Towns*, first published in 2018. They traveled one hundred thousand miles via their own plane plus rented cars for over four years. They devoted five pages to the American Prairie Reserve, which is located in northeastern Montana, about a two-hour drive south of Malta. The goal is to create the largest wildlife reserve in the lower forty-eight states. A few of their comments are below:

> Sean Gerrity, a native Montanan returned from a 20-year career in the 1980s and 90s in Silicon Valley to run the reserve. He heard about a scheme to restore these Montana grasslands, through the project now known as the American Prairie Reserve. In 2005, the money started to come, so the first piece of property was bought. Buying land from private owners and taking it out of ranching is part of the American Prairie Reserve's strategy. In the decade since that purchase, the organization has raised tens of millions of dollars, mainly from individual rich donors (like the Mars family, which still privately owns the Mars candy company) and used it to obtain control over more than three hundred thousand acres of land. About a quarter of that is land it has bought outright from private owners. The rest is public land on which it has taken over the lease and then taken the land out of grazing and converted it to wild use.

> Bit by bit, the parcels have been put together. Ultimately the ambition is to assemble some five thousand square miles of contiguous land, or about three million acres, roughly the size of Connecticut. This expanse will be big enough to support diverse

populations of species large and small, from prairie dogs and ferrets to bison, antelope, eagles, and wolves. Gerrity said that the sweeping scale means: "that you could stand in one place and see only prairie for fifty miles in any direction, and it would stretch another fifty miles beyond that."

A natural reserve was being created on the scale of the Serengeti National Park, in which the wildlife of the presettlement area would again prevail. All in all, the cost of assembling this land might come to $500 million, by the American Prairie Reserve's estimate.

Many of the ranchers are from families who have run cattle on their fenced tracts for generations. Most of them are politically conservative. Time is very likely on the reserve's side: decade by decade, the farm population dwindles, and more of these ranches are likely to eventually go up for sale—and the reserve hopes to be able to buy them.

Gerrity said, "This project is one hundred and eighty degrees different than the involvement of a new product in Silicon Valley, and that is immensely satisfying. If we can make something happen, it will be permanent. When you add another piece of property, you can stop and think that, one hundred years from now, people will round that bend and see that view. It will be permanent. Nothing I ever did before can last in that way."

Havre

Once on the other side of the river, my brother and I drove 79 miles on gravel road through the Bear Paw Mountains and eventually to Havre. If you think this stop has absolutely nothing to do with baseball, you are right. Our grandfather George Blake Bourne had sold his ranch in 1917 in the Sweetgrass Hills, northwest of Havre. The previous two years had plenty of rain and good crops. And the next three years were very dry, so it appears that George's timing of the sale was spot-on. He kept the mineral rights connected to the property, of which 50 percent were left to my brother and me. He moved his wife and son (our father) to Havre, where he eventually became the mayor and founded his own bank.

As a college student at Georgetown University in Washington DC, George and his childhood friend, James Edelin Hamilton, traveled to Montana the summer of 1887 to fulfill a boyhood dream. It is assumed that they took a train to St. Louis, then a steamboat from there up the Mississippi to the Missouri River and eventually ending in Fort Benton. Their final destination, Great Falls, was reached by a stagecoach, some forty-five miles south. The trip from St. Louis to Fort Benton was approximately twenty-five days.

They worked for a sheep rancher and had fully intended to return to college in Washington, DC, in the fall, but their employer went busted. Therefore, they had no money to purchase their train tickets back east. An assumption can possibly be made that they preferred the wide-open West to the work of a university classroom. Their payment for the summer of 1887 was in the form of sheep. This was the beginning of the Bourne-Hamilton Partnership. However, their sheep ranch was entirely wiped out during the winter snowstorm of 1888. Montana reached statehood in 1889.

Temperatures in January went as low as fifty-one degrees below zero. The snow bound ranges had as much as five feet of snow. There were huge losses of cattle in Chouteau County. The chinook winds melted the snow. Then there was a freeze. In order to eat, several animals such as cattle used their noses to move the snow aside, which was not as successful as sheep and horses, who would paw the snow with their feet. Steamboating started to decline in the late 1890s, which saw Fort Benton lose business to the railroads, which were growing all across the northern part of Montana. The big railways would not build spurs to the suffering towns, such as Fort Benton.

When no word was heard from the two boys in over a year, Jim Hamilton's father, John Hamilton, a bank director, and his mother went west. They found the boys digging postholes and rendering fat for a living.

Sweet Grass Hills

The sheep rancher whom they had worked for had given them a small claims shack, but that was damaged by the snow and winds that winter, so the two of them built additions, ten feet by twelve feet, to the homesteader house, in the open prairie in the Sweet Grass Hills. They used planks ten feet long and one inch thick. The peak of the roof was arched slightly to deflect the rain. A thin strip of wood, like tar paper, was nailed to the rafters. More experienced homesteaders helped them in this process. Not sure if the floor was raised or it was just plain earth. Water came from a nearby creek. A stove was purchased from a town-store, several miles away, on Route 2. Buffalo turds were the cherished fuel, but they were difficult to find in the open prairie. In addition, they were hard as rocks, so they had to be sawed or chopped apart to fit into the stove. It is unclear if they hunted animals, such as jackrabbits, porcupines, pronghorn antelopes, even buffalo. The antelope was one of the fastest animals in Montana. They have been clocked at speeds up to seventy miles per hour. Their taste is similar to venison.

Plains Indians and settlers were always pursuing the antelope, which managed to survive the sportsmen, homesteaders, and Indians. However, eventually, the Indians were moved from the open prairie to the reservations.

Homesteads

It was Mr. Hamilton who financed the two in purchasing a sheep ranch away from the Great Falls area up north in the Sweet Grass Hills, which had dramatic views of the buttes and sky. Gold Butte is 6,512 feet tall, East Butte a little taller at 6,958 feet, and Mount Lebanon at 5,807 feet. Each homestead had the laborious job of putting up the fences, which were six to seven miles around. And of course, they had to build fences in and around their home to contain the cattle and the hogs. It was estimated that one thousand to eleven hundred posts had to be dug per one mile. George and James had five different homesteads in Liberty and Hill counties. They were quickly gaining the reputation of two of the most industrious young sheep men of Chouteau county. Like the rest of the east Butte growers, they hauled their crop of wool to Chester.

The early settlers built near the margins of the hills, where springs naturally occurred. In 1806, Meriwether Lewis viewed the Sweetgrass Hills from afar and referred to them as the "broken mountains," as they were "destitute of timbers." Some of these quotes are from the Lewis and Clark Expedition as directed by President Thomas Jefferson. The President had made the Louisiana Purchase for almost the size of one third of America. And of course, Lewis and Clark were instructed to "check out" this new, huge real estate. The Hills are visible from Havre to Glacier National Park as you travel the High Line through Northern Montana. These island ranges are completely surrounded by the sea of plains and not geographically part of the Rocky Mountains to the west. All the higher peaks had at least one Native American religious site. George Bourne and James Hamilton had many memories of the North Central Montana area, which were filled with stories of Indians, soldiers, traders, and the early stockmen. The Sweet Grass Hills are northwest of Chester toward the Canadian border. This is not to be confused with Sweet Grass County, in southern Montana. The Indians were always looking for buffalo. They used these three buttes as lookouts for the herds of buffalo.

Gold was found in the middle butte in 1884, and the usual stampede came after, and so it was named Gold Butte. The prospectors soon followed in the mid-1880s. A few decades later a few prospectors were still searching for that elusive pot of gold.

As young college kids, George and Jim never had the slightest idea of what was ahead of them as they settled in a homestead out in the tall grass. This section of tall grasses was a world away from Washington, D. C. George and Jim were even learning about wolf and coyote behavior in the world that that wasn't in the college text books. Did they know a wolf travels from thirty to forty miles in one night?

Some of the ranch projects they confronted and had to learn were as follows:

1. Fences: Their homestead required about six miles, with about one post every ten feet. It was very difficult work, with the wires being attached by staples to each post, especially in the cold winter months.
2. Branding: They would heard the cows and calves in from the open prairie at the end of May, branding season. Each homestead would perform its own branding, but several families would assist in the procedure. It was common to see a runaway take off from the pack, but there was always a young cowboy who would ride off and rope the calf back in. The cows were groaning as the young calves were inside the coral. There were two teams with each

man a specialist: wrestler, brander, cutter of private parts, roper, inoculator. For each calf, the process took about two minutes. The efficiency of the teamwork was so important.

3. Hailstones: These storms would occur over the years. They were as large as baseballs and some as big as grapefruits. The latter, weighing between one and two pounds, even killed some of the cattle. Once the hailstones arrived, it is assumed that George and James went immediately to their root cellar. Eventually, hail insurance became a must. Michael Blake Bourne, great-grandson of George Blake Bourne and my son, experienced a similar hailstorm in Dallas, Texas in the summer of 2019 where his truck was dented by large hailstones. The violent change in the weather scared most people in the Sweet Grass Hills area, but James Hill, Head of the Great Northern Railroad, was constantly writing about man owning his own land. He wrote, "Land without population is a wilderness, and population without land is a mob."

4. Buffalo hunting: The Native American economy was based primarily on buffalo hunting, and the sweet prairie grass surrounding the hills attracted immense herds. The nomadic hunters had greater incentive when American traders began to accept buffalo robes in trade for "luxuries," and the buffalo began to provide more than just subsistence for the hunters and their families. The Indians pursued antelope, disguising themselves in buffalo skins. They were also called pronghorns. Hungry farmers just about wiped out the pronghorns in North America just after the turn of the twentieth century. The total population was reduced to fewer than fifteen thousand. More than one million today exist across North America.

5. Grasshoppers: Dry weather would bring on dried crops, and then the grasshoppers would swarm everywhere to the point where one could not see the sky. It was devastating for homesteaders when the first plague of grasshoppers hit their area. They became a voracious force when they chewed through a wheat crop. Many, many years later, in different parts of the state, spray planes flew in circles, constantly banking the plane to the left. Its inside wing was never more than eight feet off the ground.

Bourne and Hamilton were successful in their undertaking and within two years they had expanded their attractive ranch to some three thousand acres. At first, they lived in a log cabin with a dirt roof and received mail once a year. The Hill post office was opened in 1898, about twenty-three miles north of Chester and twenty miles south of the Canadian border, and closed in 1954. Another post office was opened in 1892 by George Bourne, in Whitlash. The population twenty-five years ago was ten people. The ranch continued to flourish adding many thousand sheep to their flock and then began raising some of the best breeds of cattle, which were Herefords and Shorthorns. Herefords were adaptable and had growth with added fertility. They have been used in beef production since the 1700s. Shorthorns were known for being heavy milkers, which translated into faster growing calves. And they adopted easily to new environments.

However, there were several severe storms in the Sweet Grass Hills causing quite a loss among newly shorn sheep. The only serious sheep loss reported so far because of cold and wet weather, is that of Bourne and Hamilton, who lost 190 head just after shearing. In June 1913, a bunch of Mexican sheep shearers came to Chester to go to the big ranches to shear the woolies. Typically, each adult sheep is shorn once each year. The excess wool impedes the ability of sheep to regulate their body temperature. What transportation they used to go from Mexico to Northern Montana is still a mystery. It also led to collecting buffalo bones off the prairie for shipment east, which turned out to be a prominent business for some. It was reported in the local paper that on half-breed coulee, there was a pile of bones 175 feet long, 50 feet wide, and 8 feet high, ready for transportation. Another article in the local newspaper wrote that a woman was kicked on the chin by a mule, causing her to bite off the end of her tongue, and her husband several times since refused the offer of one thousand dollars for the mule.

Chester

This was followed by a thriving general mercantile business in Chester where Bourne-Hamilton purchased a trading post for seventeen thousand dollars. A few months later, they had a large building put up near their trading post to be occupied as a saloon. Their general store took advantage of the need for fencing wire on the open prairie. Some railroad cars standing on the railroad sidings were usually full with wires to satisfy the demand. The new enterprise would not interfere with their sheep investment, in which they continued to extend their operation. And within a few years, the Bourne and Hamilton store was rated as one of the leading mercantile establishments of northern Montana. When the Great Northern Railroad arrived in 1909, the whole town was forced to move to the south side of the tracks in order to straighten a bend in the tracks. This was to the advantage of Bourne and Hamilton, who had 37 acres of their land converted into town lots. Bourne and Hamilton sold their trading store in 1909. On February 4, 1909, there was a supper at the Prairie Inn in Chester for 50 cents a plate, plus a fine for not wearing a mask. James Hill, the head of the railroad, continued to promote homesteading, which meant his railroad pleased most of the corporations, the homesteaders owned their land, and the increase in the production of food satisfied everybody. He offered to transport people to the Northwest for just ten dollars if they would farm near his railroad. He imported cattle and gave them to the settlers to lure them to the area. Hill looked forward to these farming communities achieving economic success. Then his railroad would do the same. He solved the problem of going 125 miles farther west through the Rockies by finding the Marias Pass near Glacier National Park. The pass traverses the Continental Divide along the boundary between the Lewis and Clark National Forest and the Flathead National Forest.

State Legislature

George Blake Bourne's interests were not confined to livestock, for he served, at age twenty-nine, in the state assembly in 1897 as a member of the house from Chouteau County. He was reelected to the seventh session of the Legislature in 1901. He then served as senator from old Chouteau County in the eighth session in 1903. It was once the largest county in the Montana Territory and the second largest in the United States. It was subdivided repeatedly to form other counties, until it reached its present size, an area of 3,936 square miles and a population of 5,738. When running for reelection, George was criticized by his opponent for the expensive house he had built on the ranch. It was the first house erected with a bathroom upstairs that had running water. He had his new house built in 1901 for about $10,000, and most importantly to lure Rosalie from Washington, DC, to northwestern, Montana. The interior hardwood was shipped all the way from Ohio. The house had carbide lights with a fireplace in the living room. It had eight large rooms and two baths. George was considered a spendthrift by his political opponent in the campaign. Senator Bourne was reelected for the ninth session in 1905. During this period, he was also Sheep Commissioner under Governor Smith. His friendships and acquaintances were extensive, among many classes of people. It was determined in 1913 that the water in Hill near Bourne's ranch was some of the better water in all Montana. This brought interest in lots for sale in Hill County.

Marriage and New Ranch House

George married Rosalie Marie Brawner from Washington, DC, in 1901. Their wedding trip took them around the world, stopping off in Hawaii, Europe, Egypt, and other places. During their visit to the Holy Land, Rosalie obtained a bottle of water from the River Jordan and brought it back to Montana. This water was used to baptize their only son, James Edelin Bourne. He was named after James Edelin Hamilton, George's longtime partner and foster brother since childhood.

Indians constantly came to the ranch and of course gravitated toward the new "mansion." They would camp right around the house and sometimes on the porch. Brother Jim was told a story by our parents about the several Chesapeake Bay retrievers that our grandfather had on the ranch. The Indians, with the help of the several dogs, were rounding up the cattle one afternoon. However, the dogs strayed a bit to the Indians' tepees and ate all their food, which was warming over the low fires in the tepees. The Indians returned to see that their lunches had been eaten by the dogs. They told Grandfather that they were going to cook the dogs over the fires and eat them for lunch unless he did something about it. He came up with a solution that calmed the Indians down and prevented them from going on the proverbial warpath. And peace had returned once again to the Bourne-Hamilton ranch.

Rosalie was not too interested in having many squaws sit around all day, so she had a halfway house built down from the main house. The Indians could speak English if they wanted to, but usually said, "*Namoya,*" which meant, "can't speak."

During the first decade of the twentieth century, the ranch continued to grow. Bourne purchased five thousand head of two-year-old ewes, plus Bourne and Hamilton bought one thousand head of yearling ewes. Besides the several hundred head of cattle, Bourne had been breeding Percheron horses for a number of years. They had originated in western France. They were usually gray or black, well muscled, and known for their intelligence and willingness to work. He would sell off each year the culls from the bunch, which left all his horses quite young and all high grade. When he was running all his livestock, for more than two decades, he never found it necessary to buy a single ton of hay as he always had a sufficient quantity. He used a type of grass that ranchers called strong grasses, which was good for cattle and sheep.

Bourne was spending more time each year going to Havre, Montana, where he would talk about the affairs of his firm. He could talk cattle, sheep, horses, winter wheat, barley, and oats with the best of them. In the Havre Plaindealer newspaper, George Bourne was referred to as the "Whitlash Capitalist." Even though his ranch was in Hill, he was considered to be from both Hill and Whitlash.

In 1910 the ranch of 6,916 acres was assessed for $52,227 but the final price, when he sold it in 1917, was unknown. It was the highest valuation in the entire area at the time. Thousands of more acres were accumulated in the subsequent years.

While still in ownership of the ranch, he went to work in the banking business for Honorable W. G. Conrad, in about 1912, in Livingston. A year later, he became the Cashier of the Security State Bank in Havre. Business was conducted on a successful basis for several years. In 1924, the Hill County State Bank was organized to take over part of the assets of the Security State Bank, and George Bourne was elected president.

Gonzaga Prep School and University of Notre Dame

James Edelin, George's son and our father, attended the Hill School, a one-room schoolhouse in Hill County, which was halfway from Chester, Montana, to the Canadian border. He attended the one-room schoolhouse in the open prairie on the Bourne-Hamilton property, and then the public school in Havre in the sixth and seventh grade. He was then sent to Spokane, Washington, where he attended Gonzaga Prep Boarding School, which was situated adjacent to the Gonzaga University campus. After graduating from Gonzaga Prep in 1922, he attended the University of Notre Dame in

South Bend, Indiana, majoring in mechanical engineering. Edelin, as he was known, spent several summers working at the Great Northern Railroad shop, in Havre. Much of his time was working on the steam engines. His thesis in graduate school was centered on the possibility of switching from gas engine cars to diesel.

After graduating from Notre Dame in 1926, he obtained a master's degree, two years later, in mechanical engineering, at the Massachusetts Institute of Technology in Cambridge.

Mayor of Havre

In the spring of 1921, George Bourne was convinced to run for public office as the Mayor of Havre. He pledged for strict enforcement of the law and was elected on his "cleanup" platform by a majority of four to one. He received a letter written on Ku Klux Klan stationery, signed "K.K.K.," announcing that the writers were backing him in his efforts to enforce the law and bring about a moral cleanup in Havre. Numerous arrests were made for prostitution, vagrancy, drunkenness, and gambling. Several men were convicted of bringing booze into Havre from Canada. Raids were made one night in October 1922 in the "Honky Tonk" section. Mayor Bourne personally responded to the call here and supervised the raid. All these places were taken wholly by surprise, and in every place alleged to be selling liquor was seized.

On November 6, 1922, one thousand dollars was voted to be placed at the disposal of Mayor Bourne for the employing of any additional help he deemed necessary for the detection of lawlessness in the City of Havre. After many months of criticism by the citizens of Havre, Mayor Bourne and Chief of Police James Moran were congratulated for their splendid work.

In the winter of 1931, George Bourne was taken ill with a liver complication; he spent ten days at the Mayo Clinic in Rochester, Minnesota, and passed away on February 25, 1931. The man who became so familiar to people in northern Montana as a politician, stockman, and banker was paid tribute in an editorial in the *Havre Daily News*. It read as follows:

The Long, Long Trail

There is a long, long trail winding into
the mountains of the west, to be lost from
afar into the distance.

Along that trail there passes now and again a familiar figure, to disappear in
that mystery which man has never solved, the mystery which lies on the other side
of those western mountains. It is the trail which the pioneers of our commonwealth
are traveling, as the call comes to them to make the journey toward the setting sun
which complete their services among us. For us, to whom Montana and her old-time
residents have become dear over many years of life, there is sharp sorrow when, from
among our old friends, another passes into the distance over that trail with the light of
the great mystery illuminating his face. The hand of those who built the beginnings
of a state and of the many sturdy communities in the state is thinning all too rapidly.
The first era is passing and the tasks of that era are about done. Another generation is
doing the jobs of the period which follows the pioneer stage. But the men, who carved
the state out of the vacant west, are still active and constitute among us such a band
of loyal citizens of the great state as we shall never see again. Montana's pioneers were
the salt of the earth. Those of us who have known and mingled with some of their
choice spirits will always feel for them an affection and a respect which it is difficult
to adequately express. Northern Montana has this week paid its respects to one of the
most lovable of those pioneers and has watched with sorrow the passing of George
Bourne over that long trail into the mountains of the setting sun. He has gone into that
shining pass where we all someday will wander with a mysterious urge beckoning us
on. He belonged to the choice band which gallantly and calmly faced the discomforts
and dangers of a pioneer day, to build the foundations on which the next generation
might rear a great state. He belonged to that sturdy band of old timers who lived life
enjoyably, honorably and fearlessly. For his friendship we are grateful and the memory
of it will be pleasant. For his passing we are sorrowful but we know that he himself
would ask us not to grieve. For his life we have respect and to him we pay the tribute
that is due him. We can only hope that in the shining mountains of mystery into which

the long trail winds, he has found a pleasant valley where he can make a good camp for the eternity which is on the other side of the Great Divide.[3]

The *Havre Daily News* wrote an article about Jim and me on July 30, 2002, entitled, "These Brothers' Roots Are Tied to Havre. The article ended with, "Tourists during the day, baseball fans at night. Grandsons all the time."[4]

Our next destination was Medicine Hat, Canada, heading north on Route 41. After about two hours, we stopped for breakfast in Elkwater at a diner with several pickup trucks out front. Of course, we sat at the counter so we could talk with the waitress and other people. The man next to me ordered a cup of coffee, and the waitress replied "Anything else, hon?" He asked her if she called everyone that. "No," came the reply—not from the waitress but rather from the man sitting next to my brother, a man in a trucker cap.

"I'm sweetie."

"Sunshine," said the guy one stool over.

"Precious," said the woman next to him.

This scene reminded me of the commercial on TV for Denny's new slogan: "America's diner is always open." For most people who think about food at all, when they think of a diner, they think of a place with a unique personality. And this was a unique place.

An hour later we pulled into Medicine Hat to see the Blue Jays play the Great Falls Dodgers. The Blue Jays won with the help of an unusual triple play in the top of the ninth inning. The bases were loaded, and the Dodgers batter hit a one-hopper back to the pitcher, who threw to home for one out. The catcher threw to the third baseman, who tagged the runner coming from second, and then he threw to first base for the third out.

---

[3] *Havre Daily News.*
[4] *Havre Daily News.*

There was an Old Milwaukee Beer Batter promotion: an opposing player would be chosen before each Blue Jay game. If a Blue Jay pitcher struck out this player, the price of an Old Milwaukee draught beer would be dropped to $2.50 for ten minutes following the strikeout.

David Wells, former Yankee pitcher, was a member of the Medicine Hat Blue Jays Pioneer League championship team in 1982. Medicine Hat, population of sixty-three thousand, often described as an oasis in the midst of the prairies. It is located along the South Saskatchewan River in southeast Alberta. There is an incredible contemporary museum in the downtown area.

We then drove 295 kilometers to Calgary to see the Calgary Cannons play the Sacramento River Cats in the Pacific Coast League. The city has numerous skyscrapers because of the growth of oil but it is still steeped in the Western Culture that earned it the nickname of "Cowtown," evident in the Calgary Stampede, its massive July rodeo. The population is just over 1 million. Jim and I decided that approximately 550 miles from Billings, Montana, to Calgary was a bit tiring, which meant we bagged the baseball game that night and flew home the next day.

CHAPTER 7

POLO GROUNDS, EBBETS FIELD, AND CONEY ISLAND

Separated by Age, United by the Game

It was the summer of 2005, and many Americans were saying, "Take me out to the ballgame." But not that ballgame. Far from the showboating millionaires and eight-dollar beers of major league baseball, fans were heading in record numbers to the country's other pro ballparks. These were hardly the rickety stadiums of old. Even at the humblest levels of the sport, minor league teams were offering up entertainment free-for-alls, with wine gardens, hot tubs with prime outfield views, climbing walls for the kids—oh, and a few guys playing baseball in the middle of it all.

In 2004, minor league parks hosted 39.9 million fans—up 6 percent since 2000. By comparison, about 73 million people went to see major league games last year, up less than 1 percent since 2000. This year, eight new stadiums opened for minor league teams, the most in three years. This year in Texas, the Double-A Corpus Christi Hooks moved into Whataburger Field, a new complex with a separate field for Little Leaguers, a climbing wall for kids, and a swimming pool behind the right field wall (two home-run balls have already plopped into the pool). In Greensboro, North Carolina, the Class A Grasshoppers just got a stadium with a fancy brick facade and a party deck for private functions.

Teams are focusing on amenities not only because they're profitable but also because they're one of the few things they can control. Each major league club has roughly a half dozen affiliated minor league teams throughout the United States and Canada. The big-league club pays all the salaries and uniforms of the players and determines where the players will report for duty. The local owners collect revenues from tickets, concessions, and parking where it's not free.

Prices for minor league teams first started to multiply at the end of the 1990s, making headlines in 2000, when *Comcast-Spectacor*, owners of the Philadelphia 76ers and the Philadelphia Flyers, paid $34.5 million for three minor league teams in Maryland. What the early investors saw was a perfect confluence of factors: mom-and-pop team owners willing to sell low, dozens of municipalities eager to build ballparks, the increasingly prohibitive cost to families of attending major league games, and a nearly bottomless demand for cheap, local family entertainment. Savvy operators turned some of these into virtual cash spigots.

Revenue for affiliated minor league teams has risen 9 percent a year for past decade, to about $5 million this season, according to Minor League Baseball. The average minor league ticket went up 12 percent this season, nearly double the increase in the majors.

Here are some features of stadiums throughout the country:

1. Dayton Dragons (Ohio). This sixteen-year-old park has thirty luxury boxes; fans there get free massages on Fridays and Saturdays. After every Dayton homer, a dragon looming over the outfield spews flames through its mouth. Team has big waiting list for the park's 7,200 seats. Yet the team is in last place. A new stadium was built in 2000 in downtown Dayton for $22 million.
2. Memphis Redbirds. This Triple-A affiliate of the St. Louis Cardinals plays in the minors' most expensive stadium, at $72 million. The Redbirds are owned by a nonprofit foundation that funds local kids' programs.
3. Pawtucket Red Sox. McCoy Stadium, Pawtucket, Rhode Island. No mascot races here between innings. Nothing but baseball. Most fans are in Boston shirts, as they are probably Red Sox fans true to heart; plus, there is a monitor behind right field showing Red Sox games. There is a tradition that endures from 1970s: kids still "fish" for autographs by lowering small baskets (with ball and markers) tied to a rope on a pole, to the dugout. You can buy fried clam strips for seven dollars. Seats sell for four to nine dollars. Baseball's longest recorded game took place here—thirty-three innings, featuring future stars Wade

Boggs and Cal Ripken. Unfortunately for Pawtucket, the team was sold in 2018 and is moving to Worcester, Massachusetts.

4. Sacramento River Cats, Sacramento, California. This was the minor league's top draw, packing its fourteen thousand capacity with more than seven hundred fifty thousand in 2019. The national anthem is played by grade-schoolers with violins. The organization targets fans at all levels, from the businesses that rent luxury suites for as much as $55,000 a year down to the salmon taco–eating families in the $5 seats.
5. Lake Elsinore Storm, Lake Elsinore, California. This stadium features a dancing bunny mascot, and on Saturdays, a trained pig delivers new baseballs to the umpire.

Polo Grounds

As teenagers in the mid-1950s, three buddies and I would drive from Riverside, Connecticut, to games at the Polo Grounds. The three friends—Jack Gorby, Gus Teller, and Treat Walker—and I had hung around together since grammar school. We all had just graduated from high school, working a summer job and then off to college. At ages seventeen and eighteen, we would frequent a brew house, Fritz & Tom's, in Port Chester, New York, just over the border from Greenwich, Connecticut. The drinking age in New York State was eighteen, versus twenty-one in Connecticut. One evening, we saw Willie Mays play for the New York Giants at the Polo Grounds, located along the Harlem River on the upper west side of New York City at West 157th Street and Eighth Avenue. It was a unique stadium because it was elongated with very short measurements for the two foul lines: 279 feet down the left-field line and 257 feet down the right-field. Dead center was 485 feet, which is where the clubhouses and offices were located. That meant that all the players had to walk the length of the field at the end of every game to enter their locker rooms. Every other stadium in the Majors positioned the clubhouses down and behind the dugouts. Some described the stadium as the shape of a bathtub.

Only four players hit homers in straightaway center: Luke Easter, Hank Aaron, Lou Brock, Joe Adcock. It is estimated that Babe Ruth hit one 550 feet over right-center in the upper deck in 1921.

Our cheap seats were in deep left center in a section that was occupied by older men, ages forty-five to seventy-five. Our bond was formed within a few games, when it became apparent that all of us loved baseball, and the Giants were our favorite team. Capacity was thirty-four thousand.

Willie Mays

One evening on a hot summer's night in August, we snuck a few six-packs of beer to our seats. Willie Mays hit a line drive into the gap in left center toward our seats, his hat flying off his head as he was rounding second base. He was really motoring. The ball bounced off the base of the wall, and the opposing team's left fielder backhanded it and threw a bullet toward third base. Instead of sliding directly into the third base bag, Willie maneuvered a "hook slide," where his body slides to the left of the bag but his right leg is hooking his foot just on the outside edge of the bag. His body ended up on the third-base line just left of the bag. The tag was too late, and Willie was safe for a triple. The whole stadium rose to their feet. In our section, we were all standing, clapping, screaming, and slapping each other on the backs. And then our section yelled in unison, "Say, Hey, Willie!" The triple, his speed, and the hook slide all together made me realize how great he was.

In the 1954 World Series opening game, Giants vs. Indians, Vic Wertz came to the plate at the top of the eighth inning, the score tied 2–2. He hit a towering drive to dead center, which would have been a home run in any other park in the Majors. Willie Mays, a very speedy player, ran toward the wall with his back to the plate and made an unbelievable over-the-shoulder catch. A baseball writer, college professor, and baseball teammate at Iona Prep, Tom Farrell, asked Willie in the following season at Spring Training, "How would you compare that catch to others?"

Willie's response: "I don't compare them. I catch them."

To think that I was blessed with the three best centerfielders in baseball, all playing in New York City in the mid-1950s: Mickey Mantle of the Yankees (successor to Joe DiMaggio), Willie Mays of the Giants, and Duke Snyder of the Dodgers. What a pleasure to watch all three of these players, plus Joe D. They could do it all!

Dusty Rhodes, a few innings later, came off the bench as a pinch hitter for the Giants to hit a three-run pop-fly home run for the game winner. His HR traveled about 260 feet, while Wertz's drive was caught at 483 feet. As the Yankee broadcaster Mel Allen used to say, "How about that!" How could anyone forget Bobby Thomson's HR in the Polo Grounds in 1951 to win the National League pennant? All three New York teams came in first in 1951. The Yankees won the American League pennant, and the Giants and Dodgers tied for first in the National League. I was spoiled as a baseball fan in New York City because at least one of the three teams played in the World Series each year from 1947 to 1957 (except 1948). The Yankees won seven titles in those years.

The first Polo Grounds was built in 1883 in Central Park between 110th and 112th streets and west of Fifth Ave. This area of Central Park was known for holding polo matches in the past, which explains the field's iconic name. But polo was never played in future structures built in the early 1900s. The final version was built for the New York Giant baseball team, which was their home from 1891 until they moved to San Francisco in 1957. The Yankees played all their home games from 1913 to 1923 at the Polo Grounds. The Yanks won their first World Series defeating the Giants in 1923. It was torn down in 1964 by construction workers who wore Giants jerseys in honor of their former team.

Coogan's Bluff was a hill located over the top of the final location of the Polo Grounds between Harlem and Washington Heights. Around the turn of the century, some fans would watch the games for free from their horses and carriages. To get to the ticket booths, fans walked down a long stairway from the top of Coogan's Bluff. The ticket booths served as the entrance to the upper deck, making the Polo Grounds the only major league ballpark where fans walked down flights of stairs rather than up to get to the upper deck. The restored stairway was built by the former teams that used the field: football's Jets and Giants, the Yankees, the Mets, and the San Francisco Giants. It remains the only evidence of the Polo Grounds today and is considered a city historic landmark and the last remaining relic of one of baseball's most storied ballparks.

My wife and I visited the top of the stairwell in October 2019 but decided not to walk the estimated eighty stairs straight down. This hundred-year-old wooden stairway has been replaced by a more decorative and safer wrought-iron version. It is today a large housing complex.

Ebbets Field

Another unique baseball stadium in New York City was Ebbets Field in Flatbush, Brooklyn. Built in 1913, the average attendence was thirty-two thousand the last twenty years before the Dodgers departed for Los Angeles in 1957. The Dodgers won the National League pennant in 1941 to meet their crosstown rivals, the New York Yankees, in what became known as the Subway Series. Rabid Dodgers fans were seen walking around Brooklyn with signs: "Our bums won" or "Morder dem Yanks." The Dodgers were ahead 4–3 in the ninth inning when Hugh Casey threw strike three on Tom Henrich, only to be dropped by Dodgers catcher, Mickey Owen. It was a sharp breaking curveball in the dirt, which permitted Henrich to go to first base. The Yanks subsequently went on to score four runs to win the game, and they would eventually win the World Series four games to one.

Jackie Robinson made his debut in major league baseball in April 1947 in Ebbets Field. Local musicians started the SYM-PHONY Band, which played there at every game from 1939 to 1957. They purposely played off-key. Their favorite song was played when the umpires gathered on the field to discuss a controversial play: Three Blind Mice. Dodgers announcer Red Barber used to say that they did not play music; they just made a lot of noise.

Other characters at every game: Gladys Gooding became baseball's first full-time organist. Hilda Chester sat in the bleachers and made lots of noise with her cowbell. The presence of these colorful fans brought a "down home" feeling into the stadium in the 1950s.

I personally regret having never watched a game in person in Ebbets Field. As a Giants and Yankees fan, traveling from Riverside, Connecticut, farther into Brooklyn seemed like going to a remote state. Big mistake on my part. But true to form, as a loyal Giants fan, I was indeed a Brooklyn Dodgers hater.

Charles Hercules Ebbets was co-owner from 1897 to 1902 before becoming majority owner of the team until his death in 1925. On opening day, it was realized that the owners forgot to build a press box. It was placed in the first two rows of seats in the upper deck in left field, which hung over the playing field.

The hearts of Brooklyn residents were broken when the Dodgers departed for California. Team owner, Walter O'Malley was so hated when he left with the team that the running joke in Brooklyn in 1958 was as follows: "If you were stuck in a room with Adolph Hitler, Joseph Stalin, and Walter O'Malley and you've got a gun with two bullets in it, who do you shoot? The answer: O'Malley twice.

Brooklyn Cyclones

Minor league baseball coming to Brooklyn: The Brooklyn Cyclones had a new stadium built in 2001 alongside the boardwalk in Coney Island. The Key Span Park, costing $39 million, 6,500 seat-gem opened to a sellout crowd.

Fast-forward the story to August 24, 2015. I was invited to watch the Cyclones by their play-by-play radio announcer, Stuart Johnson. It was carried on station WKRB, 90.3 FM. After an hour and fifteen minutes on the N Line subway to Coney Island, I was sitting next to Stuart with a headset listening to his descriptive comments of the Brooklyn Cyclones versus the Hudson Valley Renegades, both teams in the New York-Penn League. The Cyclones were an affiliate of the NY Mets and the Renegades an affiliate of the Tampa Bay Rays. Hudson Valley overcame a 2–1 deficit, scoring three runs in the top of the seventh to win 4–2. My seat was high up and right behind home plate. There were no homers or any good defensive plays but I had spectacular views of the Atlantic Ocean, the famed parachute drop, and the Cyclone roller coaster just beyond the left-field wall. This Mets farm club was all about marketing good old-fashioned summer entertainment at a good price.

I could have had a famous Nathan's hotdog or even frog's legs. After all, we were at the edge of the Atlantic Ocean. Craft beer was also available from the Brooklyn Brewery, around the corner. But I was more than satisfied sitting in the broadcast booth with Stuart, watching my favorite game.

CHAPTER 8
GETTYSBURG, PENNSYLVANIA; TENNESSEE; AND VIRGINIA

The Storytelling Center of America

Early in August 2003, on our way to northeastern Tennessee, we decided to stop off in Gettysburg, Pennsylvania, to see the famous Cyclorama painting in the Gettysburg museum. In the late 1880s, French artist Paul Philippoteaux took brush to canvas and created the Battle of Gettysburg Cyclorama painting. He spent months on the battlefield researching the battle with veterans, a battlefield guide, and a photographer. It took Philippoteaux and a team of assistants more than a year to complete the painting. The result is a breathtaking canvas that measures 377 feet in circumference and 42 feet high—longer than a football field and as tall as a four-story building. Jim and I viewed the painting from a circular platform. The oil painting, along with light and sound effects, immerses visitors in the fury of Pickett's Charge during the third day of the Battle of Gettysburg. A guide showed us where the artist painted himself leaning against a tree with his musket close by. In the 1990s, art conservationists repaired unstable sections of the canvas and restored details lost during previous conservation attempts.

Sevierville

The next day, we drove 500 miles down the western side of Virginia to Sevierville, Tennessee. Part of the trip was on the Blue Ridge Parkway, where one can view mountains that appear dark blue when seen at a distance. Within a few hours, the weather turned from sunny to showery, with fog that occasionally rolled across the parkway. Even on a cloudy day, the Blue Ridge Parkway is spectacular. Fog, clouds, and mist lend a moody, painterly aspect to the mountains.

We pulled into the parking lot of Smokies Park to see the Tennessee Smokies of Sevierville play the Carolina Mudcats both of the Double-A Southern League. The new park was completed in April 2000 with seating capacity of six thousand and a construction cost of $19.4 million. It is south of Knoxville and has a wraparound open concourse. The seats are above the field level, as in so many new stadiums recently. We paid four dollars for admission, two dollars for a hot dog, and three dollars for Cracker Jacks. We missed one-dollar Hot Dog Mondays. There was a speed pitch booth—one dollar for three throws. As a former pitcher, I was very tempted! However, wisdom prevailed over enthusiasm, as my orthopedic would not have approved.

The Smokies' batting coach was Steve Balboni who played parts of his eleven seasons in the major leagues with the Yankees, Kansas City, Seattle, and Texas. He hit so many tape-measure home runs with the Yankees that the sportswriters in New York City started calling him Bye Bye Balboni. David Wells pitched for the Tennessee Smokies in 1984 and 1986 and was eventually a successful pitcher for the Yankees. Managers Earl Weaver and Tony LaRussa both got their start with this franchise as well.

Rick Ankiel

Ankiel was on the roster of the Smokies as a pitcher, called up by the St. Louis Cardinals in August 1999. He was the first player since Babe Ruth to both start a postseason game as a pitcher and hit a home run in the postseason as a position player. Ankiel had a very unusual career in baseball history. He lost his ability to pitch in the middle of a playoff game due to the yips. He had a great record when, for no apparent reason, he lost the ability to throw strikes. He often threw the ball over the catcher's head to the backstop. He was released by the Cardinals the following spring. He tried all kinds of physiological therapy and even tried drinking vodka at his locker before pitching. He made a comeback five years later as a successful hitter/outfielder. Yips are thought to be connected to performance anxiety. Several golf players attended Mayo Clinic a few decades ago to cure their yips while putting. Sensors were attached to their brains and chests but the answer to the problem was not produced. Jose Altuve, all-star 2nd baseman for the Houston Astros, has the yips presently(Oct 2020) as he periodically throws the ball over the 1st baseman's head/glove.

This story reminded me of Chuck Knoblauch, second baseman for the Yankees in the late 1990s. He was a proven infielder who, after several years, developed the yips and could not throw the ball to first base. Four women in their thirties standing in the first row of the mezzanine opposite first base held up a sign that said, "Hey, Chuckie, do you want to get lucky?" I actually saw this as my season tickets were near first base, next to the Yankee dugout.

Yadier Molina

The opening of the game saw the leadoff hitter single to left field, and on the next pitch to the second batter, the Smokies catcher threw the runner out attempting to steal second base. The next pitch was another single to left field. The count went to two balls and one strike (a hitter's count) on the third hitter when, on the next pitch, the same catcher caught the runner leaning off first base, throwing him out from his knees. Jim and I looked at each other as if to ask, *Who is this guy?* We both dove into our programs to check the starting lineup and identified the catcher as Yadier Molina, age twenty-one, five foot eleven, 187 pounds, and born in Puerto Rico. He was selected by St. Louis in the fourth round of the 2000 amateur draft. His two older brothers, Bengie and Jose, were already playing in the major leagues. The St. Louis Cardinals called Yadier up the next year, and the rest is history. He recently signed an extension of his contract in 2013—$75 million for five years.

Fast-forward to October 7, 2019, the Cardinals-Braves playoff series: Molina was now thirty-seven years old. He singled in the eighth inning to tie the game. Then, in the tenth inning, he drove in the winning run with a sacrifice fly to the warning track in left field to even the series at two games each. It was another illustration to prove that Yadier is a clutch hitter. He was so pumped up that he carried his bat as he ran to first base and then threw it into the outfield as his teammate scored the winning run, much to the approval of the roaring fans in St. Louis.

Molina's batting average for the past fifteen years with the Cardinals is .282, which is unusually high for a catcher. He is widely considered one of the greatest defensive catchers of all time. He is first among active catchers with 845 assists, 41.69 percent of runners caught stealing, and 55 pickoffs. Cardinals manager Mike Shilt said, "Yadi is an elite, special player."

Catcher

Catching has become a very difficult position. The pitchers are bigger and stronger and throw much faster pitches. Plus, they are throwing more breaking balls, and they will spike a curveball into the dirt with a runner on base. This is indeed dangerous because the catcher may fail to block the pitch. Wild pitches and passed balls are common. The coaches develop a game plan that lists the tendencies of each hitter. This is part of the analytics that creates mental strain for the catcher. He must learn additional information for each player of each new team. Notice, in between pitches or batters, when he checks his wristband for more information. And the pitcher does the same within his baseball cap.

Dayton Moore, the general manager of the Kansas City Royals, said, "Catching may be the most demanding position in all sports. There are more good NFL quarterbacks, such as the star QB of Kansas City Chiefs(Patrick Mahomes) than complete catchers in the Major Leagues." Yes, throwing a runner out at second base or picking him off first base is an important asset to have, but framing has become even more important. If framing is done well, the umpire may be influenced to call close pitches as strikes as the catcher moves the pitch in his glove just a few inches closer to the plate. The only credit the catcher receives for the strikeout is unofficial credit. However, this skill is more invaluable than having the catcher improve his batting average from .234 to .275. Ken Singleton, as a broadcaster on TV, said, "Analytics puts a player in a better position to succeed." All major sports are using analytics. The major leagues made one move to help the batters after the 1968 season, when the height of the pitching mound was lowered from sixteen inches to ten inches. Now there is talk about stretching the mound one to two feet from its present sixty feet and six inches.

However, there are also new approaches to improve pitching: there are several camps in different parts of America and Canada attempting to refine the art of pitching either sidearm or submarine, making the ball sink more or upsetting the hitter's timing. Robot pitching machines are now available, but they are not yet helpful because they cannot duplicate the sinker. The first time I stepped into the batter's box against a sidearm thrower, I was seventeen. His delivery was from the third-base side of the mound, which made me bail out of the box as the pitch was called a strike. There were only about ten sidearm throwers who were pitching in the majors in 2019. None of them could throw above ninety miles per hour. That is why this approach is going nowhere. Two successful sidearm pitchers were Dan Quisenberry and Kent Tekulve. The knuckleball specialist is also fading away. The pitching coaches want *speed* in the majors.

Good all-around catchers, like Yadier Molina(St. Louis Cardinals) and Salvador Perez (Kansas City Royals), are not being developed today. Bryce Harper, arguably the second-best outfielder in baseball, was a catcher as an amateur. I wonder why he switched to the outfield? Mike Trout of Los Angeles Angels is rated number one.

Today's game(10/7/19 was called in the second inning due to rain, so we drove into town to see the statue of country singer Dolly Parton, a native of Sevierville. Population: 16,716.

Jonesborough

The Great Smoky Mountains National Park was only a short drive away, but we decided to make our way to Jonesborough, stopping off in Greenville for gas. We drove by a church on Main Street that had a sign in front: "Your confession will not surprise God." A half hour later, we arrived in Jonesborough, the state's oldest town. Around 1973, a Grand Ole Opry regular Jerry Clower spun a tale over the radio about coon hunting in Mississippi. And a teacher Jimmy Neal Smith had a sudden inspiration: Why not have a storytelling festival right in northeast Tennessee? On a warm October weekend in 1973, in historic Jonesborough, the first National Storytelling Festival was held. Decades later, the *Atlanta Journal Constitution* wrote, "In our age of fast-moving technology, it seems unlikely that thousands of audience members could spend a weekend mesmerized by the voices of storytellers. But that's exactly what happens in Jonesborough, Tennessee every year during the first weekend of October."

The *Los Angeles Times* wrote, "What New Orleans is to Jazz, Jonesborough is to storytelling."

Giving a Speech

As Jim and I strolled down the brick sidewalks, we came across live music and storytelling. On one corner, a man was talking about how to make a violin. It got me thinking of the man I had heard speak at Speaker's Corner in the far northeast corner of Hyde Park in London in 1959, about safecracking. I decided to wing it as I grabbed a microphone on the other corner: I started with the idea that expert safecrackers really can get through just about any lock mechanism. It's a matter of having the right tools, the right skills, and plenty of patience. One needs some picks, which are long, thin metal pieces with curved ends of different shapes for different types of locks and a tension wrench, which can be any tool used to create tension, including a flathead screwdriver. When picking a pen-and-tumble lock, put the tension wrench in the keyhole and turn it as if it were a key.

After a slight pause, I looked around to see that my audience was increasing to about fifteen people. Then I realized that there was a cop standing off to the left. Was he going to arrest me for my conclusion? I got nervous considering the possibility that someone might want to ask me questions when I finished. So I decided to end my comments, saying, "While you are applying pressure, lift the pins one at a time using a pick. You should hear or feel a click each time a pin falls into position."

I tried to get a little dramatic after speaking the last sentence, bending over with the mike next to my ear. I turned and whispered to Jim, "Let's get out of here." As we walked briskly up a side alley, my thoughts were of the safecracker in London who had no shirt on in July but had tattoos all over his upper torso, including his bald head and face. Needless to say, in 1959, his image was really weird, but it sure was interesting.

A few interesting facts about the state of Tennessee:

1. More Civil War battles were fought in Tennessee than any other state except Virginia.
2. The name comes from Tanasie, the name of a Cherokee village.
3. The Tennessee River flows through the state twice.
4. It is thirty-fourth largest state in the United States.
5. Its length is 482 miles.

Elizabethton

The next morning, we drove through Johnson City, the birthplace of Davy Crockett, then another half hour northeast to Elizabethton, Tennessee. In the early twentieth century, Elizabethton became a rail hub, served by three different railroad companies. That day, we commented to each other that we were becoming more touristy by the day, while we remained baseball fans at night. It seemed to us that once we moved away from the East or West Coast, everyone we met just loved America. They were all so patriotic.

We attended a game of the Elizabethton Twins and the Johnson City Cardinals in the Appalachian League (Rookie). The Twins were affiliated with the Minnesota Twins and the Cardinals with the St. Louis Cardinals. The Appy League had ten member clubs and liked to boast of players Eddie Murray, Nolan Ryan, Cal Ripken, and Kirby Puckett who started their Hall of Fame careers here on the "road to the show." Traveling around our wonderful country watching the national pastime: What more could two old men like us want in life? Dagwood Bumstead called the game of baseball "the core of our civilization."

But the minor league industry realized it had to attract nonbaseball fanatics. So, they began to sell the game as a wholesome night out with the kids, with a little baseball thrown in. In many parks around the country, the performance appears to be inspired more by Walt Disney than Abner Doubleday. The town of Elizabethton and its Little League came up with a nice patriotic idea: and sure enough, before this game, the local Little League team came swarming onto the field to take a bow and stand alongside of each Elizabethton Twins player as the national anthem was being played. Can you imagine what a thrill that must have been for each Little League player?

"Take Me out to the Ball Game"

Once the seventh inning came around, everyone in the stadium rose to sing "Take Me Out to the Ball Game." I was wondering how the song originated. I went to Google in search of information:

It was written in 1908 by Jack Norworth, the songwriter who wrote "Shine on Harvest Moon" among many others. "Take Me Out to the Ball Game" was the most popular song of that year. Norworth had never been to a baseball game, but at the age of twenty-nine, the inspiration came from a billboard while riding the subway in New York City. It read, "Baseball Today—Polo Grounds."

The first verse was sung by Gene Kelly and Frank Sinatra in 1927 in the musical film *Take Me Out to the Ball Game.* Bing Crosby included the song in an album. Carly Simon was part of the PBS documentary when she sang it for the series *Baseball* by Ken Burns. But it didn't appear in major league games until 1934. Harry Caray, the announcer for the Chicago White Sox, started singing the song during the seventh-inning stretch in 1941, with fans within earshot of his broadcast booth occasionally joining in. Caray started singing the song in 1976 over the White Sox stadium PA system, and it became a local tradition. He switched to calling games for the Cubs in 1982 and brought this tradition with him. Soon after, variations on this tradition were adopted at other stadiums. It is the unofficial anthem of North American baseball.

Most baseball fans only know the lines that make up the chorus:

Take me out to the ball game,
Take me out with the crowd,
Just buy me some peanuts and Cracker Jack,
I don't care if I never get back.
Let me root, root, root for the home team,
If they don't win, it's a shame.
For it's one, two, three strikes, you're out
At the old ball game.

A composer friend of Norworth, Albert von Tilzer, who had also never attended a baseball game, completed this music. They were both part of Tin Pan Alley, which meant that they had the experience.

Back to the action of the game. It went through both lineups inside of forty-five minutes, each team able to scratch out one hit apiece. At the top of the fourth inning, the first three batters for the

Johnson City Cardinals singled. Then the runner on third base stole home, and the other runners advanced. But they could not score again, as the Cardinals wasted a golden opportunity. The game went another three innings with no score, and the fans became enthralled with the mascots dancing on the dugouts, hugging babies, and tossing hot dogs wrapped in tinfoil up into the stands. One Tennessee Vols Hound Dog mascot was racing tiny tots around the bases. Of course, the mascot always lost. The Twins' first batter in the bottom of the ninth hit a double into the left-field corner. The next two batters went down swinging, and the third batter hit a bullet down the left-field line, striking the foul pole for a dramatic walk-off home run. The local fans jumped up and down, screaming in delight. The Twins players came pouring out of the dugout, running to home plate to greet their new hero. And of course, the fireworks were displayed soon after.

Bristol, Virginia or Tennessee

Twenty-five miles north is Bristol, Virginia or Tennessee. That was our destination to see another game in the Appalachian League. Have you ever been in a town that is split between two states? The state line runs right through the middle of downtown Bristol, Virginia, and Bristol, Tennessee.

The population of the Virginia side is 17,341, while 26,626 live on the Tennessee side of Bristol. It is home to one of the world's greatest and most popular NASCAR racetracks, the Bristol Motor Speedway, which seats in excess of one hundred fifty thousand. It has a thirty-six-degree NASCAR-banked track. Music also gives Bristol a universal appeal, as the city holds the honor of being named the birthplace of country music by US Congress in 1998.

We saw the Bristol White Sox play the Pulaski Blue Jays. The game was decided in the bottom of the ninth inning, with Bristol edging out a victory 4 to 3. Jerry Hairston, former outfielder/infielder in the major leagues from 1998 to 2013, was the manager of the Bristol team. He also played four seasons in the Mexican League. With the Chicago White Sox, he is the all-time leader with eighty-seven pinch hits. That night, he made many changes in the ninth to break the tie to score one run. The ninth man in the order was due to lead off but a pinch hitter was substituted and promptly singled up the middle. A pinch runner was sent in. The next batter bunted down the third baseline, which moved the runner to second. Then the runner was picked off second base. The manager almost lost his cool in the dugout, throwing his hat down on the floor of the dugout and stomping on it. The next batter took the first two pitches for strikes when Hairston made an unusual move by sending up another pinch hitter, who promptly hit a laser into centerfield, which hit the top of the wall and ricocheted toward left field along the wall. Both outfielders collided as they were pursuing the ball, and the hitter was now rounding third base and coming into home plate, standing up with the winning run.

We had breakfast the next morning in town, at Mother's Diner. A few specials: Kraut and wieners with two vegetables for $3.95. Slawdog for $1.25. There was a sign on the wall underneath a Coca-Cola clock that said, "This clock will never be stolen. The employees are always watchin' it."

CHAPTER 9
CAPE COD, TOLEDO, COLUMBUS, AND CHILLICOTHE

Aaron Judge Played Here

The Cape Cod Baseball League prides itself on being the oldest, most successful amateur baseball league in the nation. With roots dating back to 1885, the Cape League has helped foster the careers of thousands of top baseball players, including stars such as Hall of Famer Mickey Cochrane and Jason Veritek. The latter name sounds more like some new piece of technology from Silicon Valley. The league claims that more than one thousand of its former players have gone on to play in the major leagues.

Aaron Judge, my favorite Yankee player in 2018, played in the Cape League in the summer of 2012. It is curious that he chose a league on Cape Cod because he grew up in California and his college team was Fresno State. He is six foot seven and 282 pounds. He hits for average, hits line drive home runs, steals bases, and has an accurate arm from right or left field. He is a very disciplined player and has already developed into the team leader.

Bourne, Massachusetts

In order to play in the Cape League, potential players must have NCAA eligibility recurring at the start of each Cape League season. It is a nonprofit league that costs more than $600,000 per year to finance (league activities and operations). The league is dependent upon yearly grants, donations, and corporate sponsors. Each of the ten franchises must raise an additional $100,000–$400,000 per year to run their own individual organizations. Seventeen families in the Bourne area opened their homes to the Braves players and coaches.

89

The only game in the Cape Cod College league we saw was in Bourne, Massachusetts and of course, we had to drive over the Bourne Bridge to see the Bourne Braves play. There was a strange scene as we parked near the baseball diamond: dozens of men standing behind the backstop (cage) with radar guns pointed toward the opposing pitcher. These were scouts for major league teams following every move this six-foot-seven pitcher made. Some had their laptops, looking like oversized consultants or CIA men. They were all there just to see how fast he could "bring it up." He pitched five flawless innings, with a ninety-five-mile-per-hour fastball and an off-speed curve ball at eighty-one miles per hour. He was doing at the college level what many major league pitchers dream of: disrupting the timing of the hitter.

A *New York Post* sports writer once wrote, "He made a fast ball disappear into the night." Once he departed the game, all the scouts headed for the parking lot. However, it was not unusual to see a big pitcher with a ninety-five-mile-per-hour heater.

Evan Longoria went "yard" over the left-field fence for the opposing team, the Chatham Athletics. Longoria has been arguably the best player of the Tampa Bay Rays for the past five years in the American League East division. But he was traded recently to the San Francisco Giants.

Advice from the Stands

Throughout the game, there was an older woman in the stands, constantly yelling in a critical manner at the home-plate umpire. This reminded me of the Little League baseball story, which goes like this: At one point during a game, the coach called one of his nine-year-old baseball players aside and asked, "Do you understand what cooperation is? What a team is?"

"Yes, Coach," replied the little boy.
"Do you understand that what matters is whether we win or lose together as a team?"
The little boy nodded in the affirmative.
"So," the coach continued, "I'm sure you know, when an out is called, you shouldn't argue, curse the umpire, or call him an asshole. Do you understand all that?"

Again, the little boy nodded in the affirmative.

The coach continued, "And when I take you out of the game so that another boy gets a chance to play, it's not a dumb-ass decision or that the coach is a shithead, is it?"

"No, Coach."
"Good," said the coach. "Now go over there and explain all that to your grandmother."

Kody Clemens, the youngest son of Roger Clemens, a sophomore and first baseman at the University of Texas, signed on to play for the Bourne Braves in the summer of 2017. He hit .305 for the Longhorns this season, along with a team-leading 12 home runs and 49 RBIs. He was a fifth-round draft pick of the Houston Astros in 2015 but elected to go to college instead of signing.

The most exciting news for the Bourne Braves is the construction of a brand-new field, to be located at the Upper Cape Tech. It will have an outstanding view of the Bourne Bridge, but be assured that families will continue to line the left-field foul territory with their lawn chairs. History has it that only one in fourteen in the minor leagues would ever make it to the major leagues.

Toledo

The next day Jim, and I drove to Westchester County Airport to fly to Toledo, Ohio, where son, Mike, picked us up at the airport and drove right to the Fifth Third Field, built in 2002 on Washington Street, right in downtown Toledo. The city, population 287,208 as of 2010, is at the western end of Lake Erie. Toledo, the county, together with the state government, funded a $39 million stadium for the Mud Hens, a Detroit Tiger feeder. The ownership hosted several gatherings when fans made their suggestions regarding various facets of the stadium. There is an inside concourse that goes 360 degrees around the building. They had an eight-foot logo clock built as a Mud Hen.

This is a most unusual stadium, especially for a minor league team. They added a new twist for a sports arena: various art pieces in and around the stadium. The Knothole Gang, sculpted by Emanuel Enriquez, a resident of Bowling Green, is a group of four life-sized children trying to sneak a peek through the knotholes of the fence to see the batter. The figures are in bronze. Another piece of art, a unique mural, thirteen by eighty-four feet, was created by Leslie Adams of Toledo on another side of the ballpark. It feels as though you are looking into the farmer's market that was originally near that spot.

The rickety bleachers that once typified minor league ball have been replaced by luxury boxes, party decks, and even conference centers. The seating capacity is 10,300. The playing field of natural grass is fourteen feet below the ground level. This jewel of a park, which is more like an entertainment center, has helped rejuvenate a rundown section of the city. Designed to capture the spirit and excellent views afforded by the cantilevered balcony at historic Tiger Stadium, the club or balcony seats have been very popular, and all 1,200 seats were sold out the day we went. The unique feature of this new stadium is the Roost seating section in right field, which is an elevated deck sandwiched between and connected to the two warehouse buildings located in the right-field foul territory. It is reminiscent of the home run porch at the old Tiger Stadium, where the upper deck hung over the field, which would catch home runs instead of the outfielder catching the ball.

To encourage interaction between fans and players, the bullpens are located right past each dugout. Seating is extremely close to the action, similar to Fenway Park and Wrigley Field. If you are sitting behind home plate in the first row, you are closer to the batter than the pitcher is.

Mud Hens

The Toledo Mud Hens, one of the oldest Minor-League teams in the country, were the league champion of the Inter-State League in 1896 and 1897. The mud hen, also known as American coot, is a marsh bird with short wings and long legs. The team received the nickname in the late 1800s when they played at Bay View Park, which was surrounded by marshland and frequented by these strange birds. The nickname "mud hens" actually dates back to 1896 at the mouth of the Maumee River, and during recent years, it has been voted the most popular team nickname by readers of *Baseball America*.

There are several former Mud Hens in the Baseball Hall of Fame in Cooperstown, New York: Casey Stengel, Bill Terry, Joe McCarthy, Kirby Puckett, Hack Wilson, Jim Bunning, and others. Casey Stengel managed the Mud Hens from 1926 to 1932. Professional golfer Phil Michelson had a tryout in 2003 with the Mud Hens as a pitcher. Unfortunately, his fastball and curve were not up to the Minor-League standard.

Another cause of Mud Hen is *M*A*S*H*, the popular sitcom from 1972 to 1983. It was about a mobile army surgical care unit for the injured during the Korean War. Humor was the focus to escape from the horrors of the effects of combat. Alan Alda was the star actor. Corporal Klinger (Jamie Farr) was a very funny supporting actor who happened to be born in Toledo in real life. He often referenced the Mud Hens in the show. Very often, he wore a Mud Hens baseball hat. On the show, practiced cross-dressing to convince his commanding officer to give him a section-8 discharge. In one scene, he walked into the operating room in high heels. Here is some dialogue from *M*A*S*H*:

Corporal Klinger: "Colonel Potter, sir: I'm section 8, head to toe. I'm wearing a Wonder Bra. I play with dolls. My last wish is to be buried in my mother's wedding gown. I'm nuts. I should be out."

Potter: "Horse hockey! I've seen these dodges for forty years, all the tricks. Knew a private, pretended he was a mare. Carried a colt in his arm for weeks. Another fellow said he was a daisy. Insisted, we watered him every morning. No, no, Corporal. It ain't gonna go with me. Now you get out of the froufrou and into a uniform. And you stay in uniform. Dismissed!"

A few more Klinger lines:

"Holy Toledo! Either that bird hit a landmine, or you just shot down a kamikaze pigeon."

"I am going to live through this even if it kills me."

Jamie Farr, who played Klinger, was born July 1, 1934, is an American actor of Lebanese descent. He married Joy Ann Richards 1963 and has one daughter and one son. His first movie was *Blackboard Jungle*, in 1955, and he served two years in the US Army.

Our next stop was Columbus, Ohio to see the Columbus Clippers play the Durham Bulls. Ben Zobrist, batting .364 for the Bulls, made it to the show a few years later and starred as the Cubs' third baseman in the 2016 World Series. Last year, he was paid $10 million. B. J. Upton also played for the Bulls, was called up to the Majors in 2006 and is presently playing for the Toronto Blue Jays at $15.45 million per year. Ramiro Mendoza, a pitcher for the Clippers, born in Panama, won a World Series ring with the Yankees. He was later traded to the Boston Red Sox, where he won another World Series ring. Kevin Long, a coach for the Clippers, was later called up to be the batting coach for the Yankees. He later moved to the NY Mets.

The current Cooper Stadium, home of the Clippers since 2009, is a Minor-League affiliate of the Cleveland Indians with a beer garden in left field and a capacity of 10,100. It has a cemetery on either side of the stadium. Perhaps this is the reason why Huntington Park is to be built 2 miles away.

Chillicothe

The game was somewhat boring, so we departed in the fifth inning and drove south about 49 miles to Chillicothe. It was the first and third capital of Ohio. Today, it has a population of 21,725. It is real small-town America with old, beautiful homes, nicely maintained. There are eighteen original handpainted works of art on various buildings, which says it is a town rich in history and culture. Chillicothe was the name of a Shawnee clan. It is situated on the Scioto River, which flows south toward Kentucky, where it joins the Ohio River. Driving around town, we saw Story Mound, constructed by people of the Adena culture (800 BC–AD 100), which is right in the center of a downtown neighborhood. It was excavated in 1897. This mound is somewhat similar to the one we saw in South Dakota.

The railroads and the canal were prosperous at the same time in the nineteenth century. The rails ran from east to west versus the canal, which moved business north to south. In 1907, a flood damaged the canal and forced it to close.

The Chillicothe Paints play in VA Memorial Stadium. The Paint Horse arrived in North America along with Spanish explorers in the early sixteenth century. These horses became the mustang herds that roamed the continent's western half. The preference in color is for large splashes of white. The ballpark installed Field Turf playing surface, including base, mound, and home-plate areas. Following the 2008 season, the ownership announced it would become an amateur summer baseball team and join the Prospect League, an amateur collegiate summer league that required wooden bats. The team is always looking for host families to adopt Paints players for the season. They are included in family meals and activities, and the family is given two free tickets for all home games. Most of the players are not from southern Ohio.

In 2010, the Paints won their first Prospect League championship against the Danville Dans, on an eleventh-inning walk-off home run by Ian Nelson.

CHAPTER 10
SOUTH DAKOTA, IOWA, AND NEBRASKA

....

Ambidextrous Pitcher

On July 23, 2007, Jim, my son, Mike, and I all met in Sioux Falls, South Dakota. We visited the falls of the Big Sioux River in the northern part of the city. It has been a focus of life in the region since the founding of the city in 1856. It includes an observation tower and the remains of an old mill. Today, the park covers 123 acres. An average of 7,400 gallons of water fall one hundred feet over the course of the falls each second.

The city had two other attractions that did not appeal to us: the state penitentiary plus a huge slaughterhouse, with a stench not to believe. The Smithfield pork plant employs about 3,500 people and accounts for 4 percent to 5 percent of US pork production. But the reason for the growth in population for Sioux Falls in the past few decades has mainly been its ability to move credit card companies' processing centers from high-cost major cities in the northeast to Sioux Falls. Many citizens have moved from small towns in the two Dakotas to gain employment in Sioux Falls, such that the population grew 22 percent from 2000 to 2010. The population was 176,888 in 2017, with the metropolitan area at 265,653. The Missouri River splits the state north and south.

The Class A League is composed of five northern teams from Nebraska, Iowa, South Dakota, Missouri, and Minnesota. The other five are in southern states: Texas, Florida, and Louisiana. As we approached the stadium to buy tickets, we saw the sign: $125 per game, presented by Hot Springs Spa of Sioux Falls—Take a dip in the pool located in left field, called the Bird Bath. The package included four tickets, exclusive use of the spa for the entire game, five towels, ten hot dogs, then soft drinks, five peanut bags, five bags of popcorn, and your name displayed on the big video board.

Needless to say, we passed this up for three seats near first base for $5.50 per person.

The game that night was the Sioux Falls Canaries versus the Shreveport Sports. The Canaries, down 2–0 in the bottom of the ninth inning, received three straight walks. Their third baseman, Matt Imwalle, came to the plate and swung at the first pitch for a grand-slam home run to dead center field. The Shreveport center fielder never looked back. It was gone.

Promotions occur just about every night. The previous night was Native American Night. The Canaries team, plus an array of sponsors, provided free tickets to tribes across Sioux Nation as they honored their past and the heritage of Native Americans.

Our next destination was Sioux City, Iowa, which was eighty-five miles south on Route 29, a blue road, which meant we would not see any towns on our way. We opted to drive on the country roads, State Route 19, which enabled us to meet people in the small towns.

Lennox, South Dakota

Twenty miles later, we pulled into Lennox, South Dakota, a town named for Ben Lennox, a railroad official. The population was 2,330. Main Street was quite wide, with parking diagonally into the curb plus parallel parking right in the center of the street. None of us had ever seen this before. It was a typical looking small Midwestern town, with old Montgomery Ward lookalike buildings. We entered the only eatery for breakfast with four tables, three of them occupied. After several minutes, a woman in the next table said, "I suppose you are waiting for a waitress."

"Yes," I replied.
She said, "That is not the way it works here. You have to get up and get it yourself."
We had three rolls and three cups of coffee for a total of $3.25. As a New York City resident, I found the price incomprehensible.

Five minutes later, the same woman asked me where I was from. New York City was my response, and she then launched into several negative comments about Hilary Clinton, US Senator from New

York. It did not take long for all four tables to participate in this heated discussion. As we departed one hour later, you could hear the Clinton name still being used amongst the three tables.

Farther down the same country road, we drove through Centerville, South Dakota, another typical Midwestern-looking small town with a population of 879 and one high school with a total of ninety-seven students. Continuing south on Route 19, we came across a sign: Spirit Mound Historic Prairie. Out of curiosity, we walked up the path to the top of this mound. The legend of Spirit Mound. Spirit mound, or Paha Wakan, was known by tribes for miles around before the Lewis and Clark expedition ever came to the area. Lewis and Clark visited Spirit Mound on August 25, 1804. It was a sacred place to area tribes long before the first settlers arrived here from the east. Supposedly, little people with big heads inhabited the mound. The people of the Omaha, Oto, and Yanton tribes believed that the mound was occupied by these little people, who shoot arrows at any human who came near. To them, this was the "mountain of little people."

The height of the mound was 135 feet above the surrounding plain. It was 320 acres, which would be about 38 percent of the size of Central Park in New York City (843 acres). Great flocks of swallows, some said, was the reason the mound had an air of mystery. Jim, Mike, and I were not sure we could accept this story, so we departed for Vermillion, which was about five miles south. It is the eleventh-largest city in South Dakota, with a population of 10,844. It was tree lined with two-story buildings on Market Street. Before the settlers and homesteaders came in 1859, the junction of the Missouri River and Vermilion River had been the camping ground of one of the bands of the Yankton Sioux Indians for generations. Here they cultivated their little fields of corn. In summer, their tepees stood on top of the bluff to get the summer breezes, and when winter came, they moved to the bottom of the hill to get the shelter from the winter's storms. Along the bluff was the silent resting place of their deceased relatives. In 1843, John James Audubon, the famous artist, visited the Vermillion ravine to check on the abundance of birdlife. On August 8, 1844, the first white settlers to the area were a group of Mormons seeking a new home after being driven out of Illinois. In 1846, they moved to Omaha, and in 1847, they arrived in Utah.

On the edge of the city of Vermillion is the University of South Dakota, established in 1862. It is located on 276 lovely acres, total enrollment of 9,977, of which 7,435 are undergraduates. Thirty-six undergraduate degrees are offered, 62 percent of the students are female, and 38 percent are male. Twenty percent of the student body is from abroad.

By 1859 and 1860, the Yankton Sioux Indians were moved to the government lands, and Dakota Territory was opened to homesteaders. In this area, many were of Scandinavian descent. In the southwest part of Clay County, there are many Norwegian families. A little farther north, many Danish families came to file their homesteads. The Swedes settled in another part, as did the Irish and the French.

Driving south, we drove over the Missouri River and into Nebraska on State Route 15 to the town of Wayne, where the small Wayne State College was located on 128 acres, with an enrollment of 2,913 students. We decided to head northeast to Sioux City, Iowa, via Winnebago, which was on an Indian reservation. Mike turned to me and said, "I have been driving for close to half an hour and have not seen one other car." A few minutes later, a female cop pulled him over for doing seventy miles per hour in a sixty-mile-per-hour zone. She was part of the tribal police force on the reservation. He slipped his policeman's card with his driver's license to the female cop, who changed her demeanor in seconds. She asked Mike where he was from, returned his license, and wished Mike a nice day.

I decided to ask Mike about any interesting stories at his precinct in eastern Ohio in the past several months. He said, "One afternoon, on Thanksgiving weekend, we received a call at the headquarters from a lady who asked us to come to her house right away, as her husband had gone a little crazy. In ten minutes, we were in the lady's kitchen with family and guests standing around. She told us that her husband threw the turkey at her, after which he glanced off her face and hit the wall. He did it because she took the turkey from the freezer to the oven but forgot to turn the oven on two hours previous. He was arrested for domestic violence."

We crossed over the Missouri again to see the Sioux City Explorers play the St. Joe Rattlesnakes at Lewis and Clark Stadium, opened in 1993, capacity 3,800. There is nothing unusual about this ballpark. General admission is four dollars, and parking is one dollar. The rains came in the second inning, so we departed and headed south along the Missouri and crossed back into Nebraska, driving through the beautiful farm countryside.

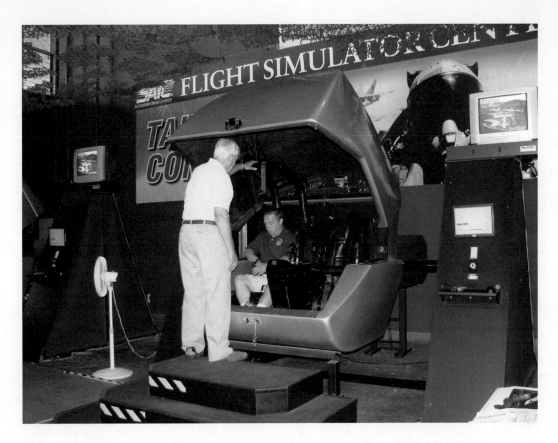

SAC Museum

Mike smartly kept the car at sixty miles per hour as we made our way to the Strategic Air and Space Museum, located halfway between Omaha and Lincoln.

The museum opened in 1959 with the mission to commemorate the aircraft of the Strategic Air Command. The museum moved to its current location in 1998 upon completion of an impressive new indoor facility, which utilizes over three hundred thousand square feet. There were B-52 bombers, stealth bombers, DC-3s, and other aircraft in several hangars, all very clean. They were well presented and very worth our while to see. It made us think that those B-52 bombers, during the Cold War, were up in the air 24/7. Mike went into a cockpit simulator that closed up and turned upside down, rolled over, and performed other motions. He had a stick in front of him that permitted him to do a barrel roll on a simulated screen. He said it was like a fully encapsulated computer game. Needless to say, Jim and I passed up this thrill.

The SAC story is more than the conflict that simmered between the US and the Soviet Union between the end of WW2 and the dissolution of the Soviet regime. The SAC story is also about scientific exploration, technological innovation, and a genuine commitment to the rigorous education and training of Americans to preserve our nation's security and enhance its prosperity. The museum has recently established a partnership with the University of Nebraska as part of this commitment to education.

It is interesting to note that the museum does not receive direct government funding and relies on the generosity of civic-minded individuals and corporations to support its programs.

Twenty minutes later, we were in Lincoln at the Haymarket Park watching the Lincoln Saltdogs versus the St. Paul Saints. Both teams are in the American Association of Independent Professional Baseball. The stadium, opened in 2001, is also the home of University of Nebraska Cornhuskers baseball team. Total capacity is 8,500, with half sitting on grass berm areas along both foul lines. The temperature around the fifth inning was 97 degrees, so we departed and drove to Omaha to have dinner at Gorat's Steak House, frequented by Warren Buffett. Nice atmosphere, but the food was overrated.

Switch Pitcher

One of the reasons I wanted to visit the state of Nebraska on our baseball trip was one Pat Venditte, an ambidextrous pitcher for Creighton University in Omaha. The *New York Times* Sports section wrote a piece entitled "Double-Barreled Pitcher Provides Shot of Confusion." Venditte, a switch-pitcher, naturally right-handed, could reach 90 miles an hour from the right side and the high 70s from the left. His deliveries are not mirrors of each other. As a right-hander, he throws over the top, with a twelve-o'clock to six-o'clock curveball. As a left-hander, he uses a whip-like sidearm delivery and a biting slider. Years ago, Yogi Berra referred to Venditte as "amphibious."

Umpires working Creighton's games have to dust off seldom-used rules regarding switch pitchers. Like everyone else, Venditte gets only eight warm-up pitches upon entering a game and five before any inning, whether he chooses to throw left-handed or right-handed and may not warm up again if he changes arms mid-inning.

A switch-pitcher facing a switch-hitter could make a fine Abbott and Costello routine. Against Nebraska University the year before, a switch-hitter came to the plate right-handed, prompting Venditte to switch to his right arm, which caused the batter to move to the left-hand side of the batter's box, with Venditte switching his arm again. To clear up the confusion, the umpires applied the rule (the same as that in the Majors) that a pitcher must declare which arm he would use before throwing his first pitch and could not change before the at-bat ended.

Venditte has a customized Louisville Slugger glove with four fingers and two webs that are flanked by two thumbs, perfectly symmetrical, so that he can slip it on either hand with ease.

Last season, he proved his ability when he used both arms in twenty-two games and struck out batters each way in twelve of them. Against Northern Iowa the previous week, Venditte quelled a third-inning rally and then, facing a lineup that alternated its lefty and righty hitters, calmly switched throwing arms ten times in the next five innings, allowing no runs and only one single.

Venditte is naturally right-handed, but his father, a former college player, noticed his three-year-old son picking up a ball and throwing it with both arms on his own. Pat Sr. cultivated that when he built a batting cage, complete with lights, near the family's home in a neighborhood of Omaha. To build his son's muscles for baseball, the father taught Little Pat to punt with both legs and throw the football with both arms.

Pat Jr. planned on attending class for his senior year at Creighton, and my brother and I, as well as my son, were hoping to see him practice on the Creighton campus. Much to our surprise, he was drafted in June 2008 by the New York Yankees in the twentieth round. He spent seven and a half years in the minor leagues, played in the majors first with Oakland Athletics, then Toronto, Seattle, Los Angeles Dodgers, and now in 2019 with San Francisco Giants for $585,000. His current team is Sacramento River Cats. He has made the six appearances over three big league seasons, during which he's posted a 5.03 ERA and 1.31 WHIP.

Having completed another interesting trip, we witnessed three games in three states, crossed over the Missouri River three times, met friendly folks, and saw unusual countryside.

CHAPTER 11

ERIE, PENNSYLVANIA, AND NORTHWEST NEW YORK

• •

A Live Rodeo in Attica

In late July 2008, Jim and I flew to Buffalo and drove about seventy miles south to Jamestown, New York, to see the Jamestown Jammers play. During the game, a man was going through the stadium interviewing the fans. It turns out that he was one of the radio announcers, and he asked us several questions. A few innings later, this same man came on the public-address system and said, "We have two honored guests from New York City: Jim and Bill Bourne, who have flown to Buffalo and driven to Jamestown to see our team play baseball. Place your hands together and welcome Jim and Bill."

That was a nice welcoming reception to the Russell E. Dietrich Jr. Park, opened in 1941, capacity of three thousand. Mr. Dietrich was a player, manager, owner, supporter, and friend of professional and youth baseball in Jamestown longer than most can remember.

The Jammers were playing Mahoning Valley Scrappers, both teams in the New York-Penn League, which was starting its seventieth consecutive season, making it the oldest continuously operated Class A league in minor league baseball. The league is comprised of fourteen clubs located in Maryland (1), Massachusetts (1), New York (8), Ohio (1), Pennsylvania (2), and Vermont (1).

Johnny Dorn was the starter for the Jammers. He was drafted in the fifth round from Nebraska University. The Scrappers starter was a six-foot-two lefty, Eric Berger, from Arizona University, who was drafted in the eighth round in 2008. They were both tagged pretty good for several runs each. Wade Korpi, Notre Dame graduate, came on in relief for the Jammers in the middle innings. He was a southpaw who threw straight over, good motion, but he also got hit a few times. Catcher Miguel Fermin, from the Dominican Republic, looked good: strong arm, good hitter but not patient as he kept swinging at the first pitch. The game was tied 11 to 11 and went into the fourteenth inning when Jimmy and I went for the exits. There were approximately fourteen college players on each team. The Jammers had an unusual promotion after the game, which we passed on. The Carlson Jewelry had a diamond dig, whereupon they would bury a diamond ring in the infield and give all ladies in attendance the opportunity to find it.

Michael Stanton

The Jammers had many players to make it to the show. To name a few: Randy Johnson, Jim Leyland, and Matt Stairs. The program had a picture on the front cover of five Jammers players who were drafted in 2007 by the Miami Marlins. None of them meant anything to me until I picked up the program again in 2017 with Michael Stanton as one of five players on the front cover. Hit fifty-nine home runs for the Miami Marlins in 2017 and was voted the MVP in the National League. He moved up to Greensboro Class A in 2008, which obviously meant that we missed seeing him in Jamestown. He opted to go pro after being drafted by the Florida Marlins. As a Yankee fan, I was ecstatic when he was traded to the Yanks in the winter of 2017.

Fast-forward the story. Stanton was interviewed by a *NY Post* sportswriter on June 21, 2018, after a Yankee game. The interview caught my eye because there was so much baseball lingo in the interview: "He fell behind in the count 0–2, Seattle pitcher tried to execute a slider that didn't slide and Stanton destroyed it for his eighth HR. Stanton said: 'You're battling there—there's a chance the pitcher could spike a few. But if he leaves one there, you've got to put the barrel on it.'"

Jamestown was named after James Prendergast, an early Chautauqua County settler. His family purchased 3,500 acres in 1806. Population, as of 2016, was 29,775. It is the hometown of Lucille Ball and Roger Goodell, the NFL commissioner. Lucy and Desi Arnaz had a museum built there in 1996. The town was once called the Furniture Capital of the World, where people visited from all over the country to attend furniture expositions at the Furniture Mart, a building that still stands in the city.

Erie, Pennsylvania

We departed for Erie, Pennsylvania, a drive of some forty-six miles to see the Erie Sea Wolves play the Reading Phillies in the Double-A Eastern League. The city of Erie, population of 98,593, is the fourth-largest city in the state. It is located in the extreme northwestern part of the Keystone state, on Lake Erie, halfway between Ohio and New York states. It was an important railroad hub in mid-nineteenth century. Being a border town, Erie was a center for transportation in the running of illicit liquor across the lake from Canada during Prohibition in the United States. Many operators "laid in a large supply of liquor before the law became effective." Speakeasies opened across the city. John Carney, author of *Highlights of Erie Politics*, noted, "About the only dry thing in Erie was the inside of a light bulb."

During the war of 1812, Commodore Perry arrived from Rhode Island to command a fleet that successfully fought the British in the historic Battle of Lake Erie, which was the decisive victory that solidified United States control of the Great Lake.

The Erie people (ERIEZ meant long tail) were native Americans living on the south shore of Lake Erie. They were destroyed in the mid seventh century by the neighboring Iroquois. An Iroquoian group lived in what is now western New York, northwestern Pennsylvania, and northern Ohio before 1658.

Presque Isle Peninsula juts out six miles into Lake Erie and forms a protective shield for the harbor of the city of Erie. There is a racetrack and casino plus a park on the peninsula. Erie Insurance is the largest employer in the area and is attempting to attract younger people to make up for the loss of workers at the large GE plant. GE continues to move workers to their Texas facilities, which has no income tax.

The Sea Wolves play in Jerry UHT Park, which was built right in downtown in 1995 for $8.7 million. A Sea Wolf is supposed to be a pirate. Our seats were in foul territory in right field, but they were aimed at the infield. The game was tied 2 to 2 in the eighth inning when Ryan Roberson, the Sea Wolves's first baseman, came to bat with the bases full of runners or "the ducks on the pond," an expression coined in 1940s by Red Barber, the popular announcer for the Brooklyn Dodgers. Roberson was six foot five and weighed 240 pounds. The first pitch was a fastball right down Broadway, and he had himself a grand slam HR. The lighthouse beyond the centerfield fence rose as is the custom when a Sea Wolf player hits one out. The crowd of 3,500 went home very happy. Jim and I stayed for another form of entertainment after the game: Cowboy Monkey Rodeo. Whiplash, the Cowboy Monkey, is a white-headed capuchin monkey that rides a Border Collie at rodeos across the country. The dog-monkey teams race at speeds up to thirty miles per hour around the baseball diamond, chasing their sheep to applause from the spectators. The Humane Society takes a dim view of strapping a monkey to a dog running around a field, but it was entertaining.

Some notables who made it to the Majors from Erie: Curtis Granderson, John Lackey, Andrew Miller, Aramis Ramirez, and Justin Verlander.

Our next destination was Batavia, New York, but we decided to take the long way via the Allegheny National Forest, situated in the foothills of the Appalachian Mountains. This national forest is somewhat off the beaten path in the extreme northwest part of Pennsylvania, but it is vast and beautiful. We stopped by to see the Kinzua Dam on the Allegheny River, which was opened in 1965. We then drove north to Warren, Pennsylvania, which is located along the Allegheny River. It is a small and quaint town of 9,244 people, where lumber was the main industry from 1810 to 1840, as the abundance of wood and access to water made it profitable to float lumber down the Allegheny River to Pittsburgh.

In 1875, David Beaty discovered oil while drilling for natural gas in his wife's flower garden. Oil came to dominate the city's economy. Many of the town's large Victorian homes were built with revenue generated by the local oil and timber industries.

We had lunch in a local eatery that had a sign on the wall as you entered: "You don't have to be crazy to work here. We train you." Maybe the owner thought he was a comedian, as there was another sign in the men's room right over the toilet: "My aim is to keep this bathroom clean. Your aim would help."

Attica's Live Rodeo

Driving farther north, I noticed Attica on the map just south of Batavia on state Route 98. We both remembered the riots of 1951. This maximum-security prison had the bloodiest revolt in the nation's history. Governor Nelson Rockefeller ordered the violent retaking of the prison by 550 state troopers and correction officers. A total of thirty-three convicts and ten correctional officers died. Prisoners were frustrated by abysmal conditions and overcrowding.

After the prison was constructed in the 1930s, it held many of the most dangerous criminals of the time: David Berkowitz, better known as Son of Sam, H. Rap Brown, and Black Panther Party leader Willie Sutton, who robbed one hundred banks. All served time in Attica.

An hour later, we pulled into the Attica parking lot, entering a side door to tell the guard that we were here to take a tour of the prison. He truly looked at us as if we were crazy, muttered a few swear words, and threw us out. We naively thought if Alcatraz Island was open to the public, why couldn't Attica be the same? Oh well—nothing ventured, nothing gained. We were in the car for half a mile when we came upon the Attica Rodeo. This was a full-fledged rodeo in the state of New York, not in Wyoming or Montana. It originally started in the late 1950s with just a fence but no bleachers. People pulled their vehicles up to the fence and sat on their hoods to watch the rodeo. It was said the second-row seating was on the roofs of the cars. There were several thousand in attendance to watch quarter horses, barrel racing, bareback riding, steer wrestling, bull riding, breakaway roping, and saddle bronc riding—all this in the little town of Attica. It was a most enjoyable two-hour visit.

Batavia Muckdogs

Soon after, we drove 20 minutes north to Batavia, population of 14,801, founded in 1801. The area's major natural resource is the surrounding agriculture land. Of course, this resource is incompatible with population growth. Massey-Ferguson was a big employer but closed down in 1956, which drove unemployment to more than 20 percent. Batavia is located halfway between Buffalo and Rochester.

Their team has one of the most memorable monikers in minor league baseball. The curiosity, of course, concerns what a muckdog actually is. Batavia is surrounded by a lot of farmland. Mucklands are fertile soil. It is dirt, but it's very dark where they grow onions on it. In fact, the area is so well known for onions that the tiny town of Elba nearly proclaims itself the Onion Capital of the World while towns like Middleburg Heights, Ohio, and Vidala, Georgia, have staked similar claims.

Feral dogs live out on the muck. It's just a cool name that sounds a lot better than the Batavian Onion Farmers or something like that. There are Muckdog teams literally all across the country.

Batavian Muckdogs sell the majority of their merchandise outside of Batavia and Genesee County to Little League teams from California all the way up to Maine.[5]

Dwyer Stadium, with a capacity of 2,600, opened in 1939. The Muckdogs were an affiliate of the Cardinals and Phillies but now are with the Miami Marlins. All dogs get in free but must be on a leash. A senior ticket was four dollars. Unfortunately, the park is showing its age in some places. There was a unique event right after the fourth inning: a lucky young fan got to hit the owner with a shaving cream pie, just off home plate.

The game was between Batavia Muckdogs and State College Spikes. The score was 0-0 by the end of the fifth inning, with both pitchers throwing bullets. After the first two batters struck out in the top of the sixth, the play by play announcer came onto the public address system and said, "This reminds me of an old Little League saying: 'Can't see it, can't hit it.'" In 2000, Phillies star Chase Utley made his pro debut with Batavia. The following year, Ryan Howard started his career with Batavia. The temperature started to drop into the low sixties and there we were without sweaters, so we headed for the parking lot. 6

6. Some of the above information was taken from The Batavia Muckdogs 2008 Program.

---

[5] Paul Caputo, "The Story Behind the Nickname."

CHAPTER 12
UTAH

· ·

Chinese Workers Connecting

In July 2009, we arrived in Salt Lake City, then drove to the Tabernacle Square, Mormon Temple, Tabernacle Choir auditorium, which is situated on thirty-five acres right in the city. Took a thirty-minute tour guided by two "sisters" of the Latter-day Saints, one from Colorado and the other from Tonga. Both in their early twenties, much to our surprise, these lovely girls were committed to converting us by having us listen to the words of the prophet, Joe Smith. The two girls were sisters for eighteen months; then they would return to their respective homes. It was a fascinating thirty minutes for Jim and me.

We returned to our parked car on a main avenue to find our car had been bumped into by a car across the way. The police officer determined that the owner of the car had forgotten to shift his car into brake mode and it just drifted across the avenue. It was indeed a bizarre accident.

The game that night was the Salt Lake Bees versus the Fresno Grizzlies, both Triple-A rated teams in the Pacific Coast League. This violated my rule of seeing only Class A–rated teams, but that decree was sometimes overruled by geography. It was scorching at the game time of 7:00 p.m.; the temperature was ninety-seven degrees, and it "declined" to ninety-five degrees at 8:30. It wasn't all that bad when you considered the background view of the beautiful Wasatch Mountains. Plus, hot dogs were $1 on Wednesdays, and General Admission was $7.50. Franklin Covey Field was built in 1994 and paid for by Salt Lake City.

Elevation at home plate is 4,229 feet above sea level, seating capacity 14,511. Don Zimmer (remember him from Elmira, NY?) was the Bees' leader around 1970. Despite his future success, Zimmer's club finished with a Salt-Lake-Pacific-Coast-League worst record of 44–99, 52.5 games behind first-place Hawaii in the Southern Division.

Salt Lake City, population of one hundred sixty-five thousand, was founded in 1847 by the Mormons, fleeing religious persecution in Illinois. Today, most of the citizens are of English, German, and Mexican ancestry. Approximately 90 percent were born in the United States. Property taxes provide most of the city's revenue.

State of Utah has population of only 1.8 million. Utah name came from Ute Indian Tribe. Beehive State stands for hard work and industry. It is eleventh largest state in US, but 33 percent is desert. Mormons are 70 percent of the population. The US government owns 66 percent of the state's land.

The next morning, we drove north to Promontory Point, stopping on the way in Brigham City, noted for its peach orchards and, of course, peach shakes. We ate breakfast at the counter in Bert's Café. We had our normal breakfast, but could not stop watching a forty-five-year-old local across from us, eating large strawberries in pancakes with whipped cream. He never came up for air, just kept shoveling it into his mouth. I wasn't sure if we were jealous or just disgusted, but we departed for another fifty-five miles northwest to Promontory Point to see the reenactment of the two railroads, Pacific and Union Pacific, meeting each other in 1869. Hundreds were dressed in period clothes to make this "short play." There was a fifty-five-year-old woman with her twenty-five-year-old daughter watching this show out on the prairie, both from Berlin, Germany. My broken German was not good enough to explain to them what the meeting of these two trains meant to the country. I learned one sentence years ago in the Hofbrau House in Munich, Germany: *Eins, Zwei, Drei—G'suffa*. One, two, three—chug (or guzzle) the beer down.

Promontory Point is near the northern part of Great Salt Lake. As the two railroad work forces neared each other in 1869 in Utah, both pushed so far beyond their railroads that they passed each other, and for over 200 miles competing graders advanced in opposite directions on parallel grades. Congress finally declared the meeting place to be Promontory Summit. After a golden spike was symbolically tapped, a final iron spike was driven to connect the railroads. Engraved on the golden spike: "May God continue the unity of our Country as this Railroad unites the two great Oceans of the world." The Central Pacific laid 690 miles of track, the Union Pacific 1,086 miles. They had crossed 1,776 miles of desert, rivers, and mountains to bind together East and West.

A diverse crew labored for Union Pacific: immigrants, ex-slaves, and Civil War veterans. They did not always get along in camp but made effective tracklaying teams.

Much of California's native workforce was trying its luck in the gold fields while Central Pacific hired thousands of Chinese workers for the job. It is estimated by some to be as many as ten thousand to fifteen thousand. Historians claim that the Chinese were willing to work on the dangerous section of the RR in the Sierra Nevada range, while the Irish and other European immigrants refused such precarious work. The tunnels were the most difficult to build in addition to being very dangerous.

The railroad changed what a pioneer was meant to be. A journey that had taken six months by ox-drawn wagon now took six or seven days by train. The Union Pacific built railroad stations along the way, and settlements grew up around them. Some railways sold supplies and even provided dormitories for emigrants until they could settle. Twenty-one years after the railroad was completed, the frontier was history.

Several miles east of the Bear River Migratory is the Bird Refuge, which has seventy-four thousand acres filled with 250 species of birds plus animals. In the short period we were there, we saw a White Pelican with huge black-edge wingspan. Others we saw: blue herons, double-crested cormorants, snowy egrets, and tons of different types of ducks. Of course, there were dozens we could not identify.

Drove to Ogden, where we saw the Ogden Raptors, owned by the Los Angeles Dodgers, play the Casper Ghosts, both Class A rated in the Pioneer League. The view beyond the outfield fence was voted by some experts as the best in professional baseball. Capacity was 6,700. We saw several peaks that eventually rise to the top of Northern Wasatch. The Raptors were down 4 to 2 in the bottom of the ninth. The first two batters walked, and the third batter hit a line drive over the first baseman's head, rolling to the wall as the two runners came into score. The second baseman took the throw from the right fielder and relayed the ball to third base with the ball hitting the runner on top of his helmet and bouncing into the stands. The umpire permitted the runner to go home, which resulted in the winning run. This reminded me of the famous radio announcer of the Chicago White Sox, Jack Brickhouse, who used to say at the conclusion of a game, "Runs, hits and errors, they are all part of the ballgame. Sometimes they help you. Sometimes they hurt you. Today they happened to hurt us."

The Pioneer League is a rookie league operating in the Rocky Mountain region and used to play teams in southern part of southern Alberta, Canada. The Salt Lake Trappers used to ride their bus for the tiresome seventeen-hour trip to Medicine Hat in Alberta. Think of how much one has to love his job to endure this long drive.

The next day, in Roy, Utah, we visited the Hill Aerospace Museum, which had a fabulous collection of planes from World War 2 and the Korean War. An hour later, we were back on the road and came upon a pickup truck with a decal on the back window: Good Old Boys with a picture of two Bucks. We then drove south of Salt Lake City to Orem, which is on Utah Lake. We toured the campus of Brigham Young University, only five miles away in Provo, Utah. Of the student body, 98.5 percent belong to the Church of Christ of Latter-Day Saints, and more than 90 percent of the football team is also Mormon. In 2016, the enrollment was 34,978.

Harry and Sydney Reed, friends from Point O'Woods, Fire Island, invited us to stay with them in Park City. Harry's daughter, Whitney Reed, greeted us at their front door to tell us that her father, still on the golf course, insisted that she introduce us to other special guests staying in the back of the house. She showed us through the living room out to their deck overlooking the back lawn. Sitting on the lawn was a huge moose with her two babies, about three months old. The mother of this large moose was born on the Reed's lawn, so she did the same with her babies after coming down from the mountains. Harry gave us a tour of Park City and Deer Valley, and we had dinner in a local restaurant. Then we departed for home in the morning.

CHAPTER 13
THE PITTSBURGH SUBURBS

Has the City Experienced a Rebirth?

On July 28, 2010, Mike met Jim and me at the Pittsburgh Airport. He told us he had driven around the parking lot a few times just before we arrived when a sheriff's deputy came up to him and asked, "Are you SWAT?"

"No, I am Special Response Team."
"Is there anything in your car that I should know about?"
Mike was a policeman in Windham, Ohio, and showed his badge to the cop.
"Out of curiosity, can I see your gear?"

"Sure," said Mike as he opened the trunk, revealing helmet, rifle, extra ammunition, three kinds of vests, handgun, taser, medical kit, night vision goggles, and slew of other equipment.

Mike was driving his large black Chevy Suburban with blue and red lights on top of his car. Secret Service, FBI, and Special Service use this identical car, which looks official. Mike said he was there to pick up his dad and uncle. During our four-day round trip of Pittsburgh, Jim was constantly kidding Mike, asking him if he was still packing his heater. Needless to say, we did feel safer the rest of the trip.

We drove north about twelve miles on Route 30 to take a little tour of the Raccoon Creek State Park. It is one of Pennsylvania's largest and most visited state parks. It has 7,572 acres with a beautiful 100-acre Raccoon Lake up near Hookstown, Pennsylvania. I asked a fisherman on the edge of the lake how he was doing. His response, "It is better than mowing the lawn."

The cemetery on the park's southwestern boundary off of Pennsylvania Route 168 is the final resting place of many of the first settlers of the area. There are 142 tombstones representing men who served in the American Revolution, the War of 1812, and the Civil War.

The creation and development of Raccoon Creek State Park is directly linked to President Franklin D. Roosevelt's New Deal plan to stimulate the economy in the 1930s and to start a sound conservation program. More than seven hundred men from the Civilian Conservation Corps worked from 1935 to 1941. There is a picturesque waterfall at the upper end of the park.

Driving south on Route 18, we stopped off at a local eatery in Burgettstown and had three cheeseburgers, one beer, and two Pepsi Colas for $18.52. The population of the town was 1,576, and it had a mayor, named Robert Linn who had been in office for fifty-eight years.

From Burgettstown to Washington, near Avella, there is Meadowcroft Rockshelter, which is a structure built on rocks providing evidence of people living in North America at least sixteen thousand years. The site provides one of the longest cultural sequences in the United States, from the earliest Paleo Indian period through the time of European settlement. Walking up many steps to the cottage, the archaeological dig is explained and how they determined how old it was.

We continued south to Washington, Pennsylvania. The town has population of 13,445, and there are thirty covered bridges in Washington and Greene counties. Google says there are eighty-eight towns in the United States with the name Washington.

The game that night was the Washington Wild Things versus Lake Erie Crushers. The Washington Wild Things are in the East Division of the Frontier League, an independent baseball league that is not affiliated with major league baseball. The Lake Erie Crushers, based in Avon, Ohio, are on the southern shore of the lake. New logos and uniforms feature grapes, a homage to Ohio's tradition of grape-growing and wine history. Most of the community believes it has to do with crushing the baseball. I researched several sources but could not find out what Wild Things meant. The only interesting tidbit I learned involved the book *Where the Wild Things Are*, written by Maurice Sendak in 1963. This is a delicate story of a solitary child liberated by his imagination. According to Sendak, at first, the book was banned in libraries and received negative reviews. Two years later, librarians and teachers began to realize that children were flocking to the book. Since then, it has received high critical acclaim.

The game was very close with good fielding and pitching on both sides. Rookie starting pitcher, Jeff Sonnenberg for the Wild Things, pitched a two-hit shutout, 2–0. Chris Sidick, in his sixth year with the club, set league career records for runs and total bases, games (497), and triples (49). He was five foot nine, weighed 190 pounds, batted left, and threw right. He came to the plate in the sixth inning, with the score tied at 0–0, man on first base with two outs. He hits a screamer down the first-base line. The ball hit the first base bag and headed near the foul line in foul territory, going all the way into the corner. Chris was now rounding second base as his teammate scored the first run. The right fielder was late getting to the ball. He picked it up and threw it to second base as Chris was approaching third base. He makes the turn at full speed, and the third base coach was frantically waving him in. He headed down the line for home plate and saw that the ball is coming from second base but up the first-base side, so Chris started a hook slide into home plate but on the third-base side of the plate as the ball arrived into the catcher's mitt, who was up the first-base side of the foul line. He lunged for the runner's body, which was on the other side of home plate. It was too late as Chris's left foot hooked over home plate to score the second run. Chris jumped up with joy as he has just completed an inside-the-park home run. He would have been called out if he had slid directly to home plate. Sidick retired from baseball two years later.

We watched this thrilling play from great seats, at $12 per, in the second row right behind home plate. There were four scouts sitting near us, only one with a radar gun, which told me there were not many pitchers in today's lineup who had a heater for a fastball.

I noticed that there was a cool ad on the back of the 2010 scorecard: "Wild Things Play with a Lot of Energy. Trust us, we know a thing or two about Energy (Consolidated Energy)."

Frank Lloyd Wright

We Drove south the next day on Route 40 to Uniontown, eating breakfast on the way at a Chuck Wagon: we all had two eggs, bacon, and toast for $4.99 per person. Eventually, we turned north on 381 for seven miles to Falling Water. We took a most interesting tour (sixteen-dollar entry fee) to see the house designed by architect Frank Lloyd Wright in 1935 for the Kaufman family as a weekend house from Pittsburgh. The Kaufmans owned the famous department store in Pittsburgh. The house sold for $155,000. It was built partly over a waterfall on Bear Run, near the town of Mill Run. The main house is 5,330 square feet, and the guesthouse is 1,700 square feet. You can see clearly how fitting the house into the landscape was more than a gimmick: with Wright's windows flung open and the creek rushing below, you experience how design and nature meld into one. Some of the furniture is built right into the house. Many shelves are attached directly into the wall, sticking out without any supports that can be seen, like the floors and terraces of the house itself. The house has the ultimate connection to nature with the modern adaptation. In 1991, members of the American Institute of Architects named the Falling Water house the "best all-time work of American architecture."

The son gave it to the Western Pennsylvania Conservancy in 1963 with $500,000 endowment. In 2009, there were one hundred twenty thousand people who took the tour at an average of $16 per person, for a total of $1.92 million. Falling Water inspired the fictional Vandamm residence at Mount Rushmore in the 1959 Alfred Hitchcock film, *North by Northwest*.

Wright designed more than 1,000 structures, 532 of which were completed. He developed a style known as the Prairie School, which strove for an "organic architecture" in designs for homes and commercial buildings. The Guggenheim Museum completed in 1959 in Manhattan on Fifth Ave and Eighty-Ninth St. is now seen by many as his masterpiece. My wife, Odessa, and I live two blocks away in the same neighborhood.

Prairie School–style architecture is usually marked by its integration with the surrounding landscape, horizontal lines, flat or hipped roofs with broad eves, windows assembled in horizontal bands, solid constructing, craftsmanship, and restraint in the use of decoration.

Wright's mentor, Louis Sullivan, believed form followed function. Wright argued that form and function are one.

Rolling Rock

On Route 711 going north, we drove through a one-horse town called Stahlstown, which had a large sign on the side of the road: We must stop Obama on Nov 2. Another eight miles and we were in Ligonier, eating lunch at the Ligonier Tavern, which was housed in a renovated Victorian home just off the central square. Outside of town is the Rolling Rock Golf Club plus Laurel Valley Golf Club. The latter was renovated by Arnold Palmer in 1988. It is a top-notch difficult course with breathtaking views of the rolling hills of Western Pennsylvania. The Rolling Rock Club is also a private club situated about fifty miles southeast of Pittsburgh. The land was owned by Judge Thomas Mellon, who left it to his son Richard Beatty Mellon and onetime president of Mellon Bank. Richard turned Rolling Rock into a rural retreat for his friends and family to hunt, fish, and ride horseback. From this, it steadily developed into an establishment that, in addition to the usual country club necessities, had stocked trout streams, duck ponds, game birds, and shooting ranges. The club also kept a pack of English foxhounds, raising pheasants and running a steeplechase from 1933 until 1983.

Twenty minutes up the road was Latrobe, where Fred Rogers was born. He was the longtime host on television of Mister Rogers' Neighborhood. Nine years later, we are all treated to the release of the movie *A Beautiful Day in the Neighborhood*, with the leading role played by Tom Hanks. If the critics today are right, Hanks is a cinch to be nominated for an Oscar, as his larger than life role. He was so good at imitating Roger's body language and speech.

Butler

We proceeded farther north to Butler, which is about thirty-five miles north of Pittsburgh to see the Butler Blue Sox play the Chillicothe Paints. The Pullman Stadium was built in 1934 and rebuilt in 2008 for $5 million. The name was changed to Kelly Automotive Park. Nearly all the Butler players live with local families in town. Blue Sox games are considered community events more than anything else. The team helps to keep kids off the streets by giving them a free ticket if they bring back two foul balls from the parking lot. Players represent colleges from as far away as Colorado and South Carolina.

We arrived just before game time to find out the game was sold out, capacity 1,400. The girl at the turnstile let us in for free after I told her we had just driven from New York City. It is a very attractive ballpark with the stands very close to the field. It is only forty feet from the home plate to the backstop, with very little room in front of the dugouts. Some players have said they like the crowd being so close. This creates a feeling of being more part of the game itself. We noticed that the distance to dead center was 425 feet, the largest in the Prospect League and larger than any major league field. Before the beginning of the game, there were helicopters and skydivers landing on the field, which was entertainment for the fans.

Chillicothe had the best record in the league, at 39–17, while the Blue Sox were 24–30. Both teams are in the Prospect League, which is a collegiate summer league where are all players must have

NCAA eligibility. There are eleven teams in two divisions in the Midwest. The Blue Sox hitters were spraying the ball all over the field. Three players had three hits apiece. Butler had a total of sixteen hits versus only five for the opponents and won easily 12–1. Kevan Smith, the starting catcher, was Butler's only former player to have made it to the Majors. He presently plays for the Chicago White Sox.

The New York Yankees had a minor league team in Butler in the 1930s and 40s. Lou Gehrig, Joe DiMaggio, and Whitey Ford all played there in the 40s. One of the games was called because the fans stormed the field midgame to get autographs. Josh Gibson also played at the park when several of the Negro teams would come through the area. This park is one of just two teams in the Prospect League to have an artificial turf infield and real grass outfield. This helps a lot in getting high school and local college games earlier in the year. There are about two hundred additional games played each year in addition to the Blue Sox.

We came to the town of Butler to see the Blue Sox play, also because I read that *Smithsonian* magazine named Butler in the top ten best small towns in America. Town was established in 1803, present population 13,369. From oil refining roots to the present-day Marcellus Shale boom, from railroad car manufacturing in the past to the headquarters of Westinghouse Nuclear today. It is the birthplace of Bantam Jeep, and Butler County is the industrial hub of the area.

The town was named after General Richard Butler, officer in the Continental Army in the American Revolutionary War. He was born in Dublin, Ireland, but moved to Lancaster, Pennsylvania, with his family. He was later removed to Mount Pleasant, Pennsylvania. He was respected and beloved by the troops, considered as an officer of superior talent. He died on November 4, 1791, from a mortal tomahawk blow at the battle of the Wabash, also known as St. Claire's Defeat, in Western Ohio.

Seeking a little diversion, we drove twelve miles south to the town of Sarver to enter the Lernerville Speedway. After almost fifty years of racing, this is still one of the top tracks in the country. It is a half-mile dirt oval track with about twelve thousand seats. I was told there would be twenty-seven heat races in nine divisions. All three of us wanted to see these races strictly out of curiosity. There seemed to be people from all walks of life in the stands, but the noise factor was huge, especially when the sprint cars went by, so we departed after forty-five minutes.

Amish

Drove some forty miles northwest to New Castle and had breakfast in the morning in a nice cozy place in New Wilmington, called Jimmies' Corner restaurant. As a result, my brother Jimmy had to pay for all three of us. We then walked around Westminster College, which was founded in 1842 related to the Presbyterian Church in the United States. It is a top tier liberal arts college with an enrollment of 1,516. Tuition and fees are $33,810. The student-to-faculty ratio is twelve to one. It is one of the oldest coeducational colleges in the nation, a pretty campus with old and new architecture.

The towns of New Wilmington and Volant are only four miles apart and are referred by some as Amish America. In New Wilmington there are 19 church districts and around 2,500 souls. Volant claims to have approximately two thousand Old Order Amish community members. There are brown top buggies and powder-blue doors on everything from homes to schools to milk houses. Plain buggies share many features with cars. Some even carry roof-mounted solar panels and GPS systems. The important part as buggies evolve, of course, is that the horse remains attended.

Amish settled the area around 1847. Volant was originally a small gristmill, incorporated in 1893. The Tavern Inn, located in the heart of New Wilmington village, was once part of the Underground Railroad during the Civil War. Main Street in Volant is a place where Amish buggies comingle with automobiles.

Twenty minutes away was Slippery Rock, home to the Slippery Rock Sliders, which played in the Prospect League. The university was founded in 1889 as a member of Pennsylvania's State System of Higher Ed. There are legends about how Slippery Rock got its name: In Colonial times, soldiers were being chased by the local Seneca Indians. The troops, wearing heavy boots, were able to cross the creek, but the Indians, wearing moccasins, slipped on the rocks in the creek bed. My memory of the name came from the announcer at Notre Dame football games in the mid-1950s, during a time-out, when he would announce several scores of other leading teams around the country and would end by saying, "Pittsburgh U. 73 and Slippery Rock University 6." The announcing of the Slippery Rock score was also added to the list of scores in 1959 at University of Michigan games in

Ann Arbor. Slippery Rock won multiple championships and had several perfect seasons in Division 2.

That evening, we attended the Slippery Rock Sliders/West Virginia Mountaineers baseball game, sitting in the first row for $7 behind home plate. As we were leaving the stadium in the third inning, their first baseman hit a towering home run over the left-center-field fence. That was a good exit for us. The team was moved to Springfield, Ohio, in October 2013 and became known as the Champion City.

Sharon/Hermitage

Moving on, we drove twenty-five miles northwest to Sharon/Hermitage, which was only five miles from the Ohio border. We had heard of the Avenue of Four Hundred Flags and decided to visit this public park, which was erected during the Iran hostage crisis of 1979 to 1981 to honor the American diplomats held hostage in Tehran, Iran. The park is on the grounds of the Hillcrest Memorial Park cemetery. Tom Flynn, the owner of the cemetery, decided on February 11, 1980, the one hundredth day of captivity, to erect one hundred flags and raise one flag every day afterward until the hostages were freed. A local steel company co-donated one hundred poles on the one hundredth day. Flynn grew tired of seeing the nation's flag being burned by Iranians on the six-o'clock news. He wanted to lift America's pride, spirit, and hope. At the end, there were 444 flags, one for each day of captivity. More than 18,000 replacement flags have flown there. One Canadian flag also flies on the avenue as a tribute to the Canadians from the Canadian embassy in Tehran who risked their lives to save six hostages from captivity.

The three of us walked under the flags for twenty minutes. It was an eerie feeling but also made us all feel very proud. How about Tom Flynn erecting all this? Even though Iran is thousands of miles away, our freedoms must never be taken for granted. It was truly a moving experience to see and hear the wind in the flags.

Mike drove Jim and me to the airport after completing four days encircling the city of Pittsburgh in some four hundred miles to see one quaint town after the other, witnessing minor league baseball games.

America's steel city was left for dead in the 1980s. Unemployment ascended big time, and the people departed in droves. However, it survived the move from manufacturing to research, health care, and software. There has been a regeneration of new skill sets. The infrastructure of bridges, highways, railroads, three rivers, and tall buildings were already in place after WW2 and have been refurbished. The cultural museums and thriving arts are alive. The Steel City has become a smart city. The rebirth appears to have been successful.

CHAPTER 14

VERMONT, MAINE, AND NEW HAMPSHIRE

Driving One Thousand Miles

My daughter's boyfriend, Chase Millard, joined my brother and me on this trip, as he was a baseball player in high school in Gainesville, Florida, and an enthusiastic fan of the Philadelphia Phillies. Chase drove 318 miles in five and a half hours from Greenwich, Connecticut, to Colchester, Vermont, which is just a few miles due north of Burlington and home of St. Michael's College, founded in 1904.

Lake Champlain

The Vermont Lake Monsters were to play the Hudson Valley Renegades in the short-season Class A Pony League. The game was played in Centennial Field, which is the oldest baseball field stadium used by a professional club in the United States. It is leased from the University of Vermont and situated on the edge of the campus. It was built in 1906 as part of the university's centennial celebrations. The Vermont University Catamounts have played at the facility on and off for a century. Seating capacity is 4,415.

The Lake Monsters are the only professional sports team in the state of Vermont. Its name pays homage to the mysterious Loch Ness–like monster that's believed to lurk in the waters of Lake Champlain, which is located west of Burlington. A Vermont Historical Society publication recounts the story and offers possible explanations for accounts of the so-called monster: "floating logs, schools of large sturgeons diving in a row, or flocks of black birds flying close to the water."

Lake Champlain is situated between Vermont and New York but partially to the north in the Canadian province of Quebec. The lake was named after the French explorer Samuel de Champlain, who encountered it in 1609. It is fed by numerous rivers and connected to the Hudson River by the Champlain Canal. Lake Champlain briefly became the nation's sixth Great Lake on March 6, 1998, when President Clinton signed the bill that was led by US Senator Patrick Leahy of Vermont. Following a small uproar, the Great Lake status was rescinded on March 24, 1998. Chances are that the two states were hoping for federal aid.

Walking into Centennial Field that evening, it created an old image of what a baseball park looked like back in the 1920s. It is as though I expected all the men to be wearing double-breasted dark suits, bow ties, and hats. There was so little clubhouse space that the Vermont Lake Monsters dress in the same room as their mascot. The dugout was so small that the entire team could not fit in. The visiting team dresses at the hotel. That said, the fans seemed to enjoy the antiquated charm. The team owner spent $2.5 million bringing the stadium up to speed.

There was a short storm in the first inning, which produced a double rainbow down the first-base line into right field and over the trees of the local houses. It was absolutely beautiful and a delightful reason to delay the beginning of the game for several minutes. The management should have passed the hat for donation to the Lake Monster players. The Vermont Lake Monsters lost 4 to 2 to Hudson Valley Renegades. Kosco, third baseman for Hudson Valley, had three hits and two RBIs, and Guillen, their left fielder, had two hits and one RBI. Vermont's left fielder, Robinson, had two hits that included a solo HR. Jamieson, the leadoff hitter for Vermont, had three hits, and their second hitter, Shipman, had two hits, but neither player had an RBI. In the bottom of the first inning for Vermont, both Jamieson and Shipman had singles up the middle, but nobody subsequently scored. The Lake Monsters left ten runners on base. They were 1 for 8 with runners in scoring position. Those two numbers usually end up in defeat.

The play-by-play announcer had a sense of humor when he recited two baseball sayings describing two pitches during the game: (1) cement Mixer, a pitch that rotates but has no movement, and (2) jack-knifing, a curveball that requires one to use his own imagination. Notable Lake Monster alumni include Jayson Bay, Milton Bradley, Orlando Cabrera, Ken Griffey Jr., Barry Larkin, Paul O'Neill, and Omar Visquel. Ken Griffey Jr. played a dozen or so games at Centennial Field just before he moved up to the show in Seattle. Attendance for the game: 3,834, tickets $5, hot dogs 50 cents.

The next morning, with Chase behind the wheel, we headed north to Jeffersonville, where our family skied for three winters at Madonna Mountain, also known as Smugglers Notch. Lily Bourne, my daughter, learned how to ski here from age two and a half to five plus. This ski mountain was built in the early 1960s by a group backed by Tom Watson, the chairman of IBM. It was an attempt to escape the crowds at Stowe Mountain. Watson's company was one of the largest employers in the state of Vermont, per a semiconductor plant built in Burlington. Several years later, IBM closed the factory, to be followed by the opening of Ben and Jerry's Ice Cream factory, built outside Colbyville.

Southeast of Jeffersonville, on Route 15, we stopped to eat in Hardwick. A full breakfast for three was fourteen dollars. Sitting at the counter, as was our custom, we found out that the owner/chef was a former minor league player. While flipping our pancakes, he was talking a mile a minute, with a deep Vermont accent, about his years in the Minors. We could not understand half what he was saying, and I think all three of us were wondering what was going to happen to our pancakes. Well, sure enough, one landed on a light fixture above our heads.

Northeast Kingdom

Farther down the road, we stopped in Danville for twenty minutes, just to walk around. One of my mother's best friends, Ginnie Bentley, from Phillipsburg, New Jersey, had a farm here for several decades, starting in the 1940s. Her son, David, was born in the house right next to ours in Phillipsburg, and we became real good friends later on in life, and shared the love of golf together. Living in the Northeast Kingdom of Vermont for several years and visiting his mother on weekends, Dave memorized several jokes with a very thick local Vermont accent. One goes like this:

Ronald Drown from Danville in the Northeast Kingdom went into the Marines. While he did his hitch there, he learned how to clean a silt trench. You do that by pouring a lot of kerosene into the trench. "Lit'er off, and when it burns out, it smells sweet as a rose, or just about." When Ronald finished his marine service, he came home to Danville. In the meantime, his father had gone "electric" at the house. No more kerosene lamps. Ronald looked at the outhouse and sure enough, it needed a good cleaning out. He figured that gas was just as good as kerosene—his father had bought a tractor and so had gas—so he poured a lot of gas down the three holes and went out the kitchen to find a match. Just then, Grandpa, feeling the need for a bowel evacuation, came out to the privy and got himself settled down with a good Sears Roebuck catalogue.

"By gawd, Ronald came back with a lit match and dripped it into one of the other hole!" Well, sir, the resultant explosion blew the roof off and blew Grandpa out. He landed in the yard, rolled over, sat up, and said, "Boy, I'm sure glad I didn't let that one go in the kitchen."

Back in 1968, Dave's mother introduced my wife and me to a Danville real estate agent because we were definitely interested in seeking out a weekend spot for skiing. This piece of real estate was really tempting: a farmhouse with four bedrooms, two barns, both double the size of the main house, 150 acres, which were half-wooded and half-open field, a wide stream running right through the property. Price: $30,000. And the skiing was only about 17 miles to Mount Burke. This was just too far away from New York City, 350 miles, which would probably take us six and a half hours each way. After lots of anguish, we eventually bought a one-room schoolhouse, converted to three bedrooms, three acres in the woods, in East Jamaica, Vermont. Price: $17,000. It took us about three hours and fifty minutes to go 223 miles. Stratton Mountain skiing was only twenty minutes away.

East of St. Johnsbury, we resumed our trip on Route 2 across the Connecticut River to Lancaster, New Hampshire, then north to Groveton. The scenery, along the Connecticut River to our left and White Mountain National Forest to our right, was just short of spectacular. Route 16 took us to Oquossoc Village in Rangeley, Maine. Oquossoc is Indian for "landing place."

Rangeley Lakes area consists of six large lakes, in addition to several ponds and waterways. This quaint, tiny town has a population of 1,168, right out of a Norman Rockwell painting. It is in northwest Maine, close to the border of the state of New Hampshire and the Canadian province of Quebec. Early explorers believed it was a land of gold and jewels discovered by the Spanish. The name may have had a Norse origin. In the town of Rangeley, there was a stream connecting Mooselookmeguntic Lake and Rangeley Lakes. The origin of the seventeen-letter word is an Abnaki word for "moose feeding place," although a humorous legend states that a Native American spotted one while hunting moose in the area. Unfortunately, we did not spot a moose, Maine's official state animal. Nor did we see a loon with chicks riding on the backs of their parents. A sign in the town of Rangeley says that Rangeley is halfway between the equator and the North Pole. I cannot imagine living between these two lakes and having to pronounce their names repeatedly to passers-bye.

We had dinner in The Gingerbread House, a charming old house which had been serving the people of the region for almost one hundred years. It has held many diverse roles in the community, from postal service via sled dogs at the turn of the twentieth century to ice cream parlor and local breakfast house in the 1950s. In 1997, it was expanded, and to this day, it is known as a fine dining restaurant for the Rangeley Oquossoc area. Today, I am told that other restaurants have moved into the area and created competition. We were served delicious meatloaf and swordfish in this homey atmosphere amongst tall pine trees and lakes.

We spent the night in Clearwater Camps, suggested to me by Billy Oppenheim, a friend and fellow worker at Alex Brown and Sons. The camp was owned and run by Tina and Mike Warren. Mike, also a fishing guide, took us out on Lake Mooselookmeguntic. The fourth largest lake in Maine, it is 132 feet deep and surface area of 25.5 square miles. Chase caught a small bass, but Jim and I were shut out. Oppenheim had a house nearby on the lake and worked in Boston. But he spent lots of time fishing for and catching brook trout. One cabin at Clearwater Camps for three of us was $150. That afternoon, Chase suggested we go for a swim in Rangeley Lake. The outside temperature was 70 degrees and partly sunny. I was reluctant at first and eventually caved in to join Chase, but needless to say, it was Northern Maine cold. The next morning, we reached Mexico, Maine, on Route 17. We had three eggs plus everything else for $4.99 per head.

Portland, Maine

Eighty miles later, we pulled into Downtown Portland, near the waterfront. We ate that night at J's Osyter restaurant, an unassuming eatery and bar on a pier. It is known for its steamed clams, mussels, oysters, and other dishes. The three of us had a "few beers" and a fair share of all the above. The steamed clams dipped in butter—wow! This joint had the reputation of being "where the locals go." It appeared as though the diversity of humanity was represented this night. Make no mistake, J's is a joint with very good seafood. We were about to depart when I realized that my brother was standing at the bar talking to a middle-aged woman. As I walked up to him, I hear her ask my brother, "Where are you from?"

He replied, "I'm a rancher from Montana."

I'm not sure how that all came about. Maybe he thought he was still on our Montana trip back in 2001.

At noontime the next day, we entered Hadlock Field to see the Portland Sea Dogs play the Harrisburg Senators. Both teams are members of the Eastern League, established in 1994. The Sea Dogs are a Double-A affiliate of the Boston Red Sox. The stadium had a seating capacity of 7,368. There is a Green Monster in left field, similar to one in Fenway Park.

My son, Mike, attended a spring baseball camp in Delray Beach, Florida, when he played for St. David's Grammar School varsity team. It was run by Bucky Dent and of course it also had their "Green Monster." Bucky Dent, not noted as a HR hitter, was playing for the NY Yankees versus the Boston Red Sox in a one-game playoff for the Eastern Division of the American League in 1978. The tiebreaker was necessitated after the Yankees and Red Sox finished the season tied for first place with identical 99–63 records. The Red Sox were the home team by virtue of a coin toss. Dent hit a three run HR over the Green Monster to help the Yankees defeat the Red Sox 5–4, and they went on to win the World Series.

Other special attractions at Hadlock Field are beyond the fence near center field: an inflatable L.L. Bean Boot and a lighthouse. The latter emerges from the ground when a Sea Dog player Goes Yard and is accompanied by a flashing light and fog. Foghorn sounds are heard as the HR hitter rounds the bases, and the lighthouse then disappears beyond the wall.

Daniel Burke, former CEO of Capital Cities/ABC, bought the Sea Dogs in 1992 when he was awarded a Double-A franchise. In 1994, he paid $3.5 million to establish the Portland Sea Dogs, a Double-A affiliate of the Florida Marlins. In 2003, Burke brought the Red Sox to Portland. Some of Boston's biggest stars came through Portland on their way to Fenway Park. The following are just a few out of more than two hundred players that have made it to the major leagues: Josh Beckett, Jacoby Ellsbury, Andrian Gonzalez, Jon Lester, Jonathan Papelbon, Kevin Youkilis, and Dustin Pedroia.

Burke had a cute idea to attract female fans to a game. Barbara Walters and Barbara Bush were special guests, and it was announced that all women with the first name Barbara would have free admission. Barbara Walters was to throw out the first pitch, but her throw did not make it halfway to home plate. It did not matter because all the fans enjoyed the presence of the two Barbaras.

The box seats for eight dollars per, near third, were fortuitous. The weather that day was seventy-three degrees and overcast. The top of the second inning for the Senators, Tyler Moore hit a home run to left field on a 2–0 pitch. In the top of the fourth, Moore singled to left field. Then left-handed Tim Pahuta hit a 0–0 pitch, a towering drive down the right-field line for a two-run HR. I am convinced it is the longest HR I have ever seen, close to five hundred feet. Our seats enabled us to watch the entire flight of the ball. It was crushed! Pahuta, the Senators' third baseman, was twenty-eight years old at the time. A Seton Hall University graduate, he was six foot four and 225 pounds. He had been playing in the Nationals' farm system for six years but never made it to the bigs. J. Howell, Sea Dogs catcher, hit a solo HR in the fourth inning on a 2–2 pitch.

This was followed in between innings with the Dizzy Bat Race. Most minor leagues teams have this fun game at least once or twice a week, where several kids are invited on the field near first base. Each kid stands near his or her bat, bends over and places his or her forehead on the bottom of the bat, then turns around and around for half a minute or more. Then a whistle blows and they all are to run to second base and then to third. Of the nine kids, some of them fell down in right field. None of them made it to second base, let alone reached third. They all acted as if they were intoxicated, and the fans roared with laughter. The Harrisburg Senators won 9 to 3.

Departing the stadium, perusing the program we saw Bryce Harper, number 34 on the roster, with a batting average of .256. It meant nothing to us at the time, but seven years later, we now know that by age twenty-six, Bryce Harper had become one of the top players in the Majors. In the summer of 2011, he made the trip to Portland but was injured.

Manchester, New Hampshire

Heading for Manchester, New Hampshire (population 112,525), my wife called me on my cell phone to say that our daughter Lily had called her, wondering what had happened to her boyfriend, Chase.

Mom: "They have been gone for four days, and he hasn't called me once. What can they be talking about?"

My response: "Would you believe it? Baseball and beer!"

In Manchester, we saw the Fisher Cats play the Harrisburg Senators. The latter played the day before in Portland. The Fisher Cats play in the Eastern League and are the Double-A affiliate of the Toronto Blue Jays major league club. Starting with the 2005 season, the Fisher Cats have played at Northeast Delta Dental Stadium. Capacity is 6,500. The Eastern League is the oldest and largest of the three Double-A leagues. It is based in Portland, Maine, and is comprised of twelve teams. The Eastern League has produced twenty Hall of Famers, with Jim Rice being the latest.

Double-A baseball has become the level where most blue-chip prospects complete their development. More and more players are jumping directly from Double-A to the major leagues while spending little or no time at Triple-A.

We watched the first part of the game from a restaurant in the Hilton Garden Inn, just beyond the left-field wall and some 425 feet from home plate. A home run was not hit our way, but we were told that the windows were shatterproof glass. It is not as exciting to sit inside and have no noise from the diamond area, so we moved outside to the stadium in the fourth inning just in time to witness the Senators' third baseman, Tim Pahuta, who had hit the huge home run the day before in Portland, miss another HR by inches as his ball hit on the top of the center-field wall for a double. The Fisher Cats tied the game in the ninth but committed errors in the tenth to give the game away to the Harrisburg Senators.

Notable players who went on to the Toronto Blue Jays were many. Here are a few names: Jose Bautista, A. J. Burnett, Melky Cabrera, Gustavo Chacin, Coco Crisp, and Todd Helton.

The city of Manchester sits on the banks of the Merrimack River. With population of 110,506, it is the largest city in Northern New England, an area comprising the states of Vermont, Maine, and New Hampshire. Kiplinger voted Manchester the second most tax-friendly city in America, second only to Anchorage, Alaska. Incorporated as a city in 1846, Manchester would become home to the largest cotton mill in the world, stretching 900 feet long by 103 feet wide and containing four thousand looms.

Chase Millard was a welcomed addition to our annual baseball trips. He fit right in as he liked hot dogs, beer, and baseball and drove the entire trip of some one thousand miles. Most importantly, he married my daughter, Lily, on October 21, 2012, and is raising three kids on a farm in West Chester, Pennsylvania.

CHAPTER 15

WISCONSIN

Capitol Building, a Treasure

Wisconsin was the next destination, in July 2012. Joe Marshall was my new traveling mate, a friend from our summer community, Point O' Woods, Fire Island. Joe was formerly an editor at *Sports Illustrated*, so he probably had forgotten more sports stories than I presently knew. Anyway, we set out from the Milwaukee airport, driving thirty-five miles northwest to see the Erin Hills golf course. The approach to Erin, Wisconsin, was on straight, flat roads until we arrived at the golf course. We were curious to see the course, as it was the sight of the US Amateur Championship in 2011, and the US Open was to be played there in 2017.

We walked around the clubhouse, ate lunch, and rode a cart to view three holes, which had us regretting not bringing our golf clubs. The championship tees are 7,735 yards, the white tees are 6,230 yards. Erin Hills is ranked number 42 on *Golf Digest's* America's 100 Greatest Courses in 2019–20. At my home course, Greenwich Country Club in Greenwich, Connecticut, the championship tees are 6,706 yards. The white tees are 6,369 yards, and both courses are hilly.

Wisconsin is America's Dairyland, estimated population of 5.5 million. More than half of the state's people are of German descent. Milwaukee is the largest city with estimated population of six hundred fifty thousand. Madison is second at two hundred thousand. There are about fifteen thousand lakes, of which Lake Winnebago is the largest.

Badgers

In 1634, the French explorer Jean Nicolet became the first white person to set foot in the Wisconsin area. He landed on the shore of Green Bay while seeking a water route to China. According to tradition, he was disappointed when Winnebago Indians, not Chinese officials, greeted him. Some of the miners lived in shelters they dug out of the hillsides. These miners were nicknamed Badgers, which, in time, became the nickname of all Wisconsinites. I always thought the state's alias was named after the animal, but the Badger was not designated the official state animal of Wisconsin until 1957. Badgers are built for digging, with squat, short-legged bodies. The hind claws are shovel-like. They are twenty-four to thirty inches in length and weigh up to twenty-six pounds. They prey on gophers, ground squirrels, prairie dogs, and snakes.

The Madison Mallards played the Green Bay Bullfrogs that evening. These teams were members of the Northwoods League, founded in 1994, a college level league similar to the Cape League. Northwoods used wooden bats, which can offer a clearer gauge of the players' professional potential. The league is comprised of two divisions, South and North—eight teams in each division—and has more teams, draws more fans, and plays more games than any other summer collegiate baseball league.

There are twenty collegiate summer leagues in the United States, which include the Alaska Baseball League.

The Madison Mallards were behind 4–2 when we arrived in the fifth inning. Derek Fisher hit a two-run homer for the Mallards to tie the score in the eighth inning. And they went on to win the game in the bottom of the ninth. There was one player from Joe's alma mater, Princeton University, who played for the Bullfrogs, plus one player from my alma mater, Notre Dame University.

Capitol Building

Joe and I took a tour the next day of the Wisconsin State Capitol Building/Rotunda, which is absolutely spectacular. The original was built in 1838, which stood for twenty-five years until it was replaced by a larger building in 1863. After a devastating fire left the second Madison Capitol badly damaged, George B. Post and Sons designed the current capitol, between 1906 and 1917, at a cost of $7.25 million. Today, it is estimated to cost $200 million to replace the present capitol.

The capitol's dome, reaching to a height of over 284 feet from the ground floor to the top of the statue, is the only granite dome in the United States, and it has the state animal, the badger, on top. The height of the capitol building in Washington, DC, is 288 feet. Madison is the only state capitol ever built on an isthmus. There is an observation deck, 100 feet high, around the base of the dome, which is situated between lakes Mendota and Minona. It houses both chambers of the Wisconsin Legislature along with the Wisconsin Supreme Court and the Office of the Governor. As we walked about the building, we were told of the forty-three varieties of stone from around the world and hand-carved furniture and exquisite glass mosaics. The architecture, art, and furnishings throughout the building were styled after the council chambers of the Doge's Palace, in Venice. One would expect to find such a grand building in Washington, DC. The people of Wisconsin must be very proud of their capitol building. The city was named after James Madison, the fourth president of the United States.

The State Supreme Court room is decorated in the German and Italian style, featuring extensive use of marble. George Post designed four proportional wings and a central dome. As we were on tour, Joe noticed that there was no security. We even entered the governor's private office while he was attending a meeting. There were probably many hidden security cameras that we were not aware of.

It was lunchtime, so we headed for a restaurant named the Old Fashioned, which was on the square facing the capitol building. They were serving fifty-two different Wisconsin craft beers, of which an estimated two hundred were rotated throughout the year. This got us to inquire about the craft beer industry, which is so popular in Wisconsin. The states with the most craft breweries are (1) California, (2) Washington, (3) Colorado (with the most breweries per capita), (4) Michigan, and (5) New York. Wisconsin is number fourteen. Beer consumption is declining nationwide, but craft brewing is still strong in Wisconsin. There are approximately five thousand breweries in America. The old beers that my friends would recognize would be Pabst Brewing, which bought Schlitz and recently relaunched "Schlitz Gusto" beer and Old Milwaukee.

After breakfast, we drove due west looking for the House on the Rock, north of Dodgeville built by Rob Jordan atop a chimney of rock, sixty feet high, opened to the public in 1959. Construction started in 1945. He built a complex of quirky, architecturally distinct rooms of a Japanese style home, plus gardens and street shops. Jordan collected unique items from all over the world. If you wanted to tour the whole compound of 2.5 acres, you would need at least five hours. A few examples: mechanical bands, the world's largest carousel with over 260 different handcrafted animals, more than 20,000 lights, and 182 chandeliers. Senior admission was $29.95.

Frank Lloyd Wright

Thirty-five miles north, we drove into Richland Center, where Frank Lloyd Wright was born in 1867. While in residence at Talesin, Frank Lloyd Wright designed the Warehouse in 1917–21 for the wholesaler Albert Dell German in exchange for unpaid bills. It was the only warehouse designed by Wright and is generally considered to resemble a Myan temple. It employs a unique structural concept whereby the building rests on a pad of cork for stability and shock absorption. Wright used concrete slabs for the floors, supported by concrete columns that grow smaller in size, proceeding upward to the fourth floor. For me, it was one strange-looking building.

Going toward the state line of Minnesota, we came across Viroqua, a charming little town in the center of one of the greatest organic farming regions of America. There is breathtaking scenery because the town is at the edge of the Ocooch Mountains.

Farther north, we entered Westby in Vernon County, the self-proclaimed "round barn capital of the world." It is a Norwegian name that literally translates to "western city." There are fifteen such barns built in the early decades of the twentieth century, some painted red, gray, brown, and blue. Most farmers are third and fourth generation. Westby Cooperative Creamery is the only plant in Wisconsin that still makes cottage cheese. More than two hundred farmers, and their families supply milk daily to the creamery and own the business.

That evening, the LaCrosse Loggers beat the Lakeshore Chinooks 8–2. The catcher for LaCrosse was a Princeton student, and Lakeshore had an outfielder from Notre Dame. There are eight colleges in LaCrosse, a city of 51,834 (2017). They are leading the city toward becoming a regional technology and medical hub. The temperature during the day reached 105 degrees, and it was 97 degrees at game time, weather unfit for any activity.

After breakfast in downtown LaCrosse, we drove across the Mississippi up the pretty western side of the river on Route 61 in Minnesota. As daytime tourists, we felt compelled to stop in Winona to see the Basilica of St. Stanislaus, a Polish church built in 1894–95. Within the diocese, it is better known as Saint Stans. It is 43,560 square feet, with gorgeous stained-glass windows and a huge pipe organ loft. Many were supposedly enamored with the beauty of the basilica, which I agree with on the inside but not the outside. It is red and grayish white with several spires. There is a small grotto outside with a statue of Our Lady of Lourdes.

The city of Winona, population 27,592 (2018), on the banks of the Mississippi, is named after legendary figure Winona, said to have been the first-born daughter of Chief Wapasha. The original settlers were Yankee immigrants from New England. It is known as the stained-glass capitol of the United States.

Another sixty miles north, we crossed the Mississippi again and eventually to Wausau in the middle of the state on the Wisconsin River where the Wisconsin Woodchucks played the Madison Mallards. The Woodchucks had won their last ten consecutive home games; plus, they had a relatively new exciting player, Eric Filia-Snyder . In his first seventeen games he was batting .397, with three home runs, seventeen runs batted in, and sixteen stolen bases. We were anxious to see Filia, but he walked in his first two plate appearances, and the Woodchucks were ahead 3–1 in the fifth inning when there was a lightning and rain delay, so we departed for our hotel.

Filia later made the jump to Seattle Mariners, but in late August 2019, he tested positive for a drug abuse for the third time. As a result, he was suspended for one hundred games. Baseball America recently rated him as having the "best strike zone discipline in the organization."

The stadium in Wausau, Athletic Park, was built in 1936. There was plenty of free parking all around the park right in the middle of a neighborhood of Wausau. It made me recall the old saying: "He went yard." This baseball lingo came from Little League games that were situated near residential houses with no fences, and the long hit would roll into a neighbor's yard for a home run.

Notre Dame vs. Iowa U.

On our way south toward Grafton, driving near Lake Winnebago, I saw a sign for the town of Neenah, which brought back terrible memories of a Thanksgiving weekend in 1957 with two classmates from Notre Dame. All three of us were invited to the home of a female friend from Barat College in Lake Forest, Illinois. We arrived in Neenah the Wednesday before Thanksgiving. The hostess's parents, plus two other Barat girls, were very gracious and friendly. Unfortunately, we had made the decision beforehand to leave on Friday. That morning, we drove some 275 miles for nearly five hours to Iowa City, Iowa. Yes, that's right—we drove all the way on a cold late November day to see Notre Dame play the University of Iowa in football.

The next afternoon at the stadium, there were snow flurries, with temperatures in the low twenties. Made us wonder why we had left those lovely girls sitting around a warm fireplace back in Neenah! Could there be three twenty-one-year-old boys who could have made such a stupid decision? Well, it only got worse, going from the sublime to the ridiculous. We snuck two six-packs of beer to our seats, which proceeded to freeze by the second half. Notre Dame lost 48–6. Iowa students broke off part of the goal post after the game ended and tried to push us off the football field and out of the stadium. We then walked into town and entered a fraternity house, where we immediately received kidding from the Iowa students. I kept thinking, *Are those lovely girls thinking of us?* The sad conclusion was they had forgotten us.

Drove to Kohler to see two very good golf courses: Whistling Straits and Blackwolf Run. Both were created by legendary golf course designer Pete Dye. They have hosted three PGA Championships and several others. In 2020, Whistling Straits will host the Ryder Cup Matches.

One year in the 1990s, I came to Kohler to play the Straits and Blackwolf Run with three friends. The former has a few beautiful holes on the edge of Lake Michigan, and there was tall grass in the ruff of most holes. Needless to say, we did stray a "few" tee shots. Our caddies, wearing white overalls as they do in the Masters, were very professional as they always located our "lost balls." Again, Joe and I should have taken our golf clubs.

Chinooks

The game that night was Lakeshore Chinooks vs. Battle Creek Bombers at a new stadium in Mequon on the scenic bluff campus of Concordia University, overlooking Lake Michigan. The Chinooks' name was taken from the Salmon Chinooks of Lake Michigan. The new field was designed with an all-synthetic infield that would serve as home to the Chinooks and the Concordia Falcons baseball teams. The Chinooks' ownership group included Bob Uecker, Hall of Fame announcer, plus Robin Yount, Hall of Fame major league player, who also played for the Chinooks in his college days in the Northwoods League. Both teams are members of this collegiate summer league.

Of all the games we saw over the course of some twenty-five years, I purchased several baseball caps, but I felt that only three were unique: the Toledo Mud Hens, the Utica Blue Sox, and the Lakeshore Chinooks; two jerseys were bought: the Bourne Braves and Gonzaga Baseball. My son was wearing his Gonzaga shirt recently in Dallas, Texas, when a graduate introduced himself. I still wear the Chinooks cap, and am asked numerous times: "What is a chinook"? There is not a simple answer. In fact, it is severalfold.

1. A member of a North American people formerly inhabiting the lower Columbia River Valley and adjoining coastal regions of Washington and Oregon. In 1805, the Lewis and Clark Expedition encountered the Chinook tribe on the lower Columbia. They were superb canoe builders and navigators, skillful fishermen, and planters.
2. A dry wind that descends the eastern slopes of the Rocky Mountains, causing a rapid rise in temperature of twenty to forty degrees that occurs in ten to fifteen minutes. The winds are caused by moist weather patterns originating off the Pacific coast, cooling as they climb the western slopes and then rapidly warming as they drop down the eastern side of the mountains. The chinook aids the railroads in keeping the tracks clear of snow, enable the stockmen to bring their cattle safely through the winter, and stores up water for future use,

making irrigation in the summer possible. The greatest recorded temperature change in twenty-four hours was caused by chinook winds on January 15, 1972, in Loma, Montana; the temperature rose from negative forty-eight degrees to forty-nine degrees Fahrenheit. Loma is situated on the Missouri River, northeast of Fort Benton.

3. Chinook salmon, which are found in Lake Michigan and the other Great Lakes.
4. A baseball team in the Northwoods College League, in Wisconsin.

"The Plight of the Chinook Salmon"

Here are some excerpts from an interesting *NY Times* article from September 17, 2019:

The Columbia River was once the most productive wild Chinook habitat in the world. Salmon are critical as a food source for animals from bears to eagles to insects. Should the four lower dams be removed? Some 45,000 spring-summer Chinook spawned here in the 1950s. The average today is about 1,500 fish, and declining.

Orcas or killer whales along the West Coast survive by eating up to 30 Chinook a day in the winter and spring, which amounts to 300–350 pounds of wild fish per day. The four Snake River dams are used primarily to create reservoirs for the barging of Idaho's wheat to ports. But the dams raise water temperatures and block travel migration routes, increasing fish mortality. However, federal agencies responsible for managing fisheries on the Columbia though, maintain that removing Snake River dams is not critical to the survival of salmon and that hatchery-reared fish have made up for the loss of the River's wild fish for the orcas.

The extreme migration of the spring-summer Chinook Salmon is one of the natural world's great journeys. Before the dams were built in the 1960s and '70s, the fish born in the Middle Fork were swept by strong spring currents eight hundred miles to the sea. The rivers moved them rapidly along, and the young fish reached the brackish waters of the Columbia River estuary in a couple of weeks.

As they travel, young fresh-water salmon undergo a transformation called smoltification, becoming smolts able to thrive in saltwater. A smolt is usually a two year old salmon who is ready to migrate to the sea. After leaving the river, the fish turn north and travel to the North Pacific, near the Aleutian Islands.

They spend up to four years feeding at sea, and then those that survive the seagoing journey return to the mouth of the Columbia. Their physiological changes are reversed as they move upstream, and they again become freshwater fish. They can jump a 8–12 foot waterfall, going upstream.

The female releases clusters of eggs as the male sidle up, releasing its sperm at the same time. The current mixes them, resulting in fertilization. The eggs are adhesive and stick to the gravel after they fall. The female buries them in an egg packet. The mating is repeated multiple times, all told, some 5,000 eggs may be released by a single female. By the time she finishes, she's within a day or two of dying.

Before the Snake River, dams were built, three to six of every 100 fish that left their natal streams returned home, a ratio called smolt-to-adult return. Today, that number is just under one. Biologists say it must reach four to rebuild the fisheries.[6]

Much to my regret, I feel compelled to mention gambling because there are so many newspaper and magazine articles about sports betting. The so-called slow play in baseball seems to be the ideal sport for bettors throughout the land or in attendance at the stadium because of the pauses between pitches. Plus, the change of innings as the teams replace each other on the field or in the dugout. Of course, analytics come into play regarding the spin rate of the pitch and the velocity of the ball once it is hit by the batter. The professional bettors have access to these numbers of each player, which influences their waging. Artificial intelligence is becoming so important in the competitive business

---

[6] Jim Robbins, *NY Times*.

world. Will AI be combined with analytics to further analyze the individual baseball player? If so, then maybe robots will be placed in each dugout and bullpen. God forbid!

The state of Wisconsin is beautiful to visit, but we were cheated on the baseball because of the unusual inclement weather. We traveled approximately 950 miles in the middle of the state from the eastern border of Minnesota to the eastern border of Wisconsin on Lake Michigan.

CHAPTER 16

SPOKANE, WASHINGTON, AND NORTHWEST MONTANA

Foul Ball Knocks Beer out of Female's Hand

We landed in Spokane, Washington July 14, 2019. My wife, Odessa (Neepie) and son, Mike, were my partners for this trip to the northwest. Spokane is 92 miles from the Canadian border, 18 miles west of the Idaho border, and 279 miles east of Seattle. The population is 219,916. It is called the Lilac City for the purple blooms that thrive in the area. Spokane gets its name from the nearby Native American tribe of the same name, which means Children of the Sun in Salish.

Unusual Davenport Hotel

The unique historic Davenport Hotel was our choice for two nights. Opened in downtown Spokane in 1914, it features grand rooms like the Spanish Renaissance lobby and the magnificent ballroom, which was inspired by the Hall of Doges in Venice, Italy. During the hotel's renovation in 2000, the hand-painted frescoes, ornate woodwork, and European-inspired marble were all meticulously restored, including the genuine gold leaf around the lobby hearth. Louis Davenport had a reputation for his meticulous attention to cleanliness, and sure enough, he introduced a bonus to the clientele soon after the hotel was opened. It was washing the client's money: silver coins, and paper currency that was starched and pressed. Here is a short description of the procedure in the book: *Spokane's Legendary Davenport Hotel*, by Tony Bamonte and Suzanne Schaefer Bamonte:

The average coinage washed each day amounted to between $6,000 to $10,000. Some of the paper currency that Davenport patrons received in exchange was new. Although washing the coins was a clever, memorable gimmick, it may also have been a sanitation measure. It is a known fact that money is one of the world's most significant carriers of germs. Consequently, the clean money set the tone for the sanitary conditions one could expect at the Davenport.

The famous guest list, included, to name a few, Charles Lindbergh, Benny Goodman, John F. Kennedy, Babe Ruth, Dionne Warwick, Harry Connick Jr., Taylor Swift, and Bing Crosby.

Back to our schedule. We drove to Avista Stadium to see the Spokane Indians play the Everett AquaSox. Both teams are members of the Northwest League A short season. Everett is twenty-eight miles north of Seattle, which we visited in 1999. We saw the AquaSox play there one late afternoon and had the opportunity to see the spectacular Cascade Mountains from our reserved seats between home plate and first base.

The Spokane Indians were ahead 2–1 by end of the sixth inning, helped by a double off the right center-field wall, some 370 feet from home plate. But the AquaSox exploded for five runs in the top of the seventh, with Cash Gladfelter crushing a two-run home run. In the bottom of the ninth inning, Indians DH David Garcia hit a two-run homer, which curled around the right-field foul pole. The Everett pitcher, catcher, and manager started protesting before Garcia had rounded the bases. However, the two runs were posted on the scoreboard. The home-plate umpire and base umpire met near the pitcher's mound to discuss the issue at hand. After about five minutes, they then motioned to the Indians manager in the third-base coaching box. He then got very angry, using unpleasant language, and was ejected immediately from the game. The head umpire signaled foul ball and told the press box to delete the two runs from the scoreboard. The local fans felt cheated; they went nuts and screamed at the umpires. The next Indians' batter was called out on a contested third strike swing to end the game. He muttered something to the umpire and was thrown out of the game. This simply made the Indians' supporters even more angry, talking to themselves about the unfair umpiring as they walked through the exits.

Gonzaga Libraries

We met Corrina Kelsey the next morning in the Gonzaga Prep School library. She was in the development department of the Prep School and informed us that the school had turned coed in the 1970s and had ceased being a boarding school. As a day school, the tuition was $21,475. The present student body is from thirty-seven different zip codes. Seventy percent of students are Catholic, and 88 percent of graduates attend four-year colleges. Corrina was extremely cordial and helpful. She directed us to the Gonzaga University library on a separate campus. The old records of the high school were restored to digitized form from 1924 back to the turn of the century. The prep school and university were founded in 1887 by Father Joseph Cataldo, an Italian-born priest and missionary with the Jesuits. The university is named for the young Jesuit Aloysius Gonzaga, the sixteenth-century Italian Jesuit saint.

In 1881, Father Cataldo purchased 320 acres along the north bank of the Spokane River. 152 acres serve as the campus today. The present student population of the University is 5,091, and 875 for the high school. The latter went coed in 1975.

We walked around the campus of the high school, plus the university. Flowers throughout both campuses were well cared for and colorful. Mike and I were talking baseball as we approached the prep school's practice field. We had lunch after in the cafeteria of the university.

My sole purpose in coming to Spokane was to obtain information about my father, James Edelin Bourne, who had attended Gonzaga Boarding School in 1917 and graduated in 1922. Bing Crosby graduated in 1920. He was winner of the Academy Award for Best Actor for his role as Father Chuck O'Malley in the motion picture *Going My Way*. My own son was as enthusiastic as I was about retracing my father's footsteps in his teenage years. Mike never knew his grandfather as my father died at age thirty-eight, when I was less than five years old. His death prevented me from ever having the opportunity to discuss his school days with him.

The only vivid memory of my father was when he took my brother and me plus our Chesapeake Bay retriever down to the Delaware River in Phillipsburg, New Jersey. We rode in a 1938 two-door Ford coupe with a rumble seat, where all of us sat out back for only a mile or so to the river's edge. We threw what seemed like hundreds of sticks out into the river for our dog, Count, to retrieve.

Our research produced a photo of my father on the Debating Team, as well as his graduation photo, which showed a very studious and distinguished young man on his way to Notre Dame, and to MIT for a graduate degree in mechanical engineering.

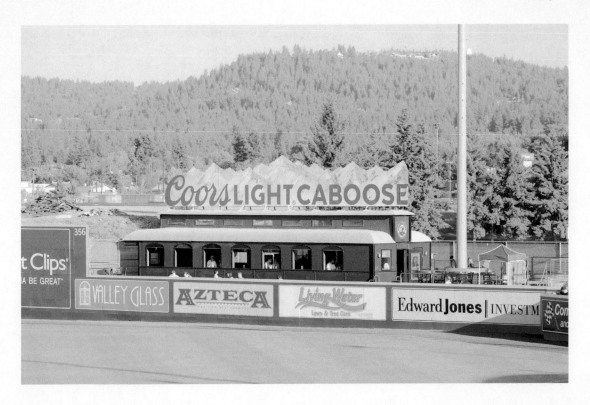

We returned that evening to Avista Stadium to see the same two teams go at it again. Tonight's game was first Responders Appreciation Night. Both teams were tied for first in the North Division of the Northwest League. As we entered the stadium, we were handed 8" × 10" placards of a red K, which were to be waved vigorously anytime the Spokane Indians' pitcher struck out an AquaSox player. This got the Indians' fans more involved in the game. The Indians were going through a tough patch of play as they had lost nine out of the last ten games. But the enthusiasm in the past two days did not wane at all. In fact, of the last twenty-five years of attending minor league games, we had not seen such an enthusiastic crowd of local fans as in Spokane. Any time an Indian player did something good on the field, you heard it from the fans. In the third inning, we saw Kellen Strahm, out of San Jose State, hit one deep over the right center-field fence and onto the roof of the Coors Light Caboose. A blast of about 395 feet! It is a replica railroad car that accommodates eighty people to drink beer, have burgers, chicken sandwiches, hot dogs, and other snacks while watching the game. It can be reserved for the night for $2,880.

In the fourth inning the AquaSox retaliated with DH Cash Gladfelter, who drove in a run with what the announcer described as a "longhorn double." The next inning, Indian catcher from Venezuela, David Garcia, led off with a walk. He proceeded to steal second and then stole third. Soon after, he scored on a balk. The game was tied until the eighth inning when the Indians' Jonah McReynolds, from Martinsville, Virginia, hit one out 370 feet. After the game, he said, "He hung that one, and I got a good swing on it." Indians 5, AquaSox 4.

Free Beer

One interesting sideline during the game was when a foul ball was hit five rows back over our heads. A Red Cross nurse rushed up the aisle right near our seats to see if someone was hurt. No one was, so she left, but a few minutes later, she returned with a free draft beer for the woman whose beer had been knocked out of her hand by the foul ball.

The view from our third-base seats beyond the field was a contrast of fairgrounds, yellow railroad cars, and beautiful green mountains. It was definitely an added treat to the baseball game. Later in the game, the moon came out just above the Budweiser sign. It was a challenge to photograph the moon just above the sign as the clouds kept moving in and out.

Otto Klein, senior vice president, came to our seats to introduce himself. We had communicated a few weeks before our arrival via the internet. He was very proud of his organization in controlling the customer service. The culture of the family was important to him in describing the generations and generations who attended games since 1903. He said that there were more attendants at his stadium than any other organization. There are 600 applicants for 150 jobs but no free tickets for the thirty-eight home games. An average attendance of 5,400 per game versus a capacity of 6,803. There are $1.50 hot dog nights with $1.00 Pepsi. I told Otto that the appreciation of the fans far exceeded any other stadium we had attended in twenty-five years.

The Dominican Republic has been a fertile area for talented young players in the major leagues for several years. The Spokane Indians have nine players on their roster from DR.

Do not miss Frank's Diner on west second St. It is a restored Pullman car with stained-glass windows. It was built in 1906 and used by the president of Northern Pacific Railroad as his private car until 1931. It was run as a diner in Seattle until 1991, when it was refurbished in 1992 and moved back to Spokane. Now, the fabulous selection of breakfast food is served on an old polished wooden countertop with inlaid design.

Missoula

Mike drove two hundred miles across the northern part of Idaho, through the beautiful Coeur D'Alene mountains into Montana. He then followed the Bitter Root mountains ending in Missoula.

That evening, we attended the Missoula Osprey/Ogden Raptors game. Our seats were opposite third base, in sight of the mountains just on the edge of the city. The stadium used to be a logging site. It was the biggest plywood factory in Missoula in 1972. J. Orocho, from Puerto Rico, started the game off for Ogden Raptors with a walk, stole second and third, and scored on a flyout. Spencer Brickhouse, six-foot-four, 235-pound first baseman, was chosen before the game so everyone could root for him. Why? Because any hit he executed, all fans could have a beer for two dollars off the price, but all the fans had to make it to the beer stand within ten minutes. Sure enough, his single in the fifth inning resulted in dozens and dozens of fans running to the beer stand.

The Raptors, whose record was 23–6 in the Pioneer League South, and who were carrying an eight-game winning streak, were just too much offense for the Ospreys to handle the night before, as Jim Titus, Andy Pages, and Sam McWilliams all went Deep for Ogden. And Titus had three additional hits. Tonight, The Raptors won again 9–6 but with only one HR. Sauryn Lao, from Dominican Republic, homered in the first inning for Ogden with one man on. F. Maxwell hit one in the fifth and Martinez one in the seventh for the Ospreys, but they were solo shots. The Raptors outhit the Osprey 12 to 9 but were only 2 for 11 with runners in scoring position. J. Reyes, infielder for the Osprey, went 0 for 5 and left five players on base.

The attendance was only 1,492, but the temperature was perfect at seventy-seven degrees with low humidity. Seats were twelve dollars per between home and third. Again, our view of the game was perfect with green mountains right behind the city with a large white *M* branded on the side of the mountain for the University of Montana. Taylor Rush, Director of Marketing, came to our seats to introduce himself. As did another officer, Matt Ellis. Taylor was informative and enthusiastic about his team and the game of baseball, as he chatted with us for twenty minutes. He thanked me for not asking for free tickets to the game, which never entered my mind.

Of the previous forty-five games we saw throughout these sixteen trips in the United States and Canada, I never predicted an individual player to make the jump to the major leagues. My one exception is Liover Peguero of the Missoula Ospreys. He was the leading hitter in the Pioneer League at .371. He was a smooth fielding shortstop with pop in his bat. He hit to all fields and had a very strong arm. He was athletic, with a great, positive attitude, and *only eighteen years young*. He looked like the real deal.

Fast-forward to 2020, when he became the sixth-ranked player in the Pittsburgh Pirates system.

Mike drove us Wednesday morning through Lewis and Clark National Forest to Helena, the capital of Montana. Walked a couple of blocks from our hotel to Bad Betty's Barbecue, which was a popular little hole-in-the-wall restaurant, where the owner was sporting a long beard with a friendly personality. He was offering racks of ribs, pulled pork, Texas-style brisket, and other barbecued delights. Everything was cooked right in front of us, and it was delicious

Sheep Industry

After lunch, we made our way to the Montana Historical Society Library, opposite the capitol building. We were introduced to Rene Massicotte, who was a tremendous help in gathering several books of history regarding the times my grandfather, George Blake Bourne, was in the State Senate from 1897 to 1905. This was thrilling for my son, Mike, because his middle name is Blake, named after his great grandfather. George was the sheep commissioner under Governor Smith. The sheep industry was precarious then because there were still countless roving bands of Indians. Development of the sheep industry waited, as did that of cattle raising and agriculture, until the state was invaded by railroads. Upon the advent of the railroad, the buffalo hunter renewed his efforts as he was given an easy way to market hides, and by 1882–83, the last buffalo was seen on the plains. Indian wars prevailed from 1870 to 1878, resulting in the creation of reservations for Native Americans.

Then with free range and with a railroad to carry the wool to market, the sheep industry of the state began to develop by leaps and bounds. Heretofore, wool was sent to market via flatboat down the Missouri or the Yellowstone to the Mississippi and on to New Orleans. And from there by steamboat to Boston.

Before dinner that night, we discovered the Brewhouse Pub to have drinks, a few blocks from our hotel and across the street from Carroll College. This school was founded in 1909 and presently has 1,342 students. It is a private institution sponsored by the Diocese of Helena, Montana. A renovation project started last year to make the library an academic hub of the college. The lead donors of the new structure are Roy and Frances Simperman of Seattle. Roy is class of 1962. The Center for Professional Communications, as part of the library, is a one-stop shop for students to strengthen their writing and speaking skills while also introducing digital enhancement to their communication skills. Digital displays, power ports, and other connections make working together electronically a seamless experience. Light and bright are the main attributes of the study spaces, with floor-to-ceiling views of the surrounding hills. The estimated cost of the project is $7 million. Its endowment was $43 million as of 2014.

At the bar, a couple to our left encouraged us to take a boat ride on the Missouri River, just off Route 15 in Gates of the Mountains Wilderness. The female bartender made the same suggestion, which was repeated by the couple to our right. So, twenty miles up Highway 15, we exited for the boat ride with about forty other people up and down the river for about two hours. There was clean, blue water, and soaring rock.

Driving Back in Time

Mike, behind the wheel again, drove us back on Route 15 heading toward Great Falls. To be a bit adventurous, we exited near Cascade onto a dirt road. We did see numerous cattle but not another car nor one human being for the next two hours and forty-five miles. We were being treated to the land of grass as our eyes were stretched out to the limits of imagination.

Where is everybody?

It was lush, green rolling prairie that I was gazing at out the window. Beautiful and blue were emphatically added to Big Sky Country, which seemed to stretch all the way to the Pacific Ocean. I am trying to envision the same countryside that my grandfather and father experienced 110 years ago. The real treasure of the Treasure State is space. And this is what we saw during our circuitous route to Great Falls. The land still flows to the horizon just the way it did in 1887 when my grandfather arrived in Great Falls. Did the tall green grass whisper in his ears as it did in mine? I certainly believe so.

The first sheep came to Montana from California in the 1870s. There were fifty thousand sheep in Meagher County, northeast of Helena. In 1880, Fort Benton became the number-one wool market in Montana. The first Montana Woolgrowers Association was started in Fort Benton in 1883. Later on, the wool was carried to the market by the railroads.

This treeless region, also known as the Northern Plains, extends north beyond the Canadian border. The plains above the Missouri River was Indian country. The Indians hunted buffalo north and south of the Canadian border, paying no attention to the political boundaries. The American farmers burned the grass near the border to make sure the buffalo roamed only south of the border. Several years before Grandfather George Bourne's and father James Bourne's time (1887–1917) in northern Montana, the area north of Fort Benton was one of the most lawless regions of the frontier. Indians shooting, coyotes, wolves, and buffalo, selling the skins and pelts to the traders, but it was whiskey and stolen horses that produced the biggest profits. Several years before Bourne's arrival, there were many rough roundups (the process of collecting the cattle by riding around them and driving them in), wild bar fights between bullwhackers and cowboys. Rodeo is a Spanish word meaning "to round up." Bullwhackers were commonly "colorful" characters and given to expressing themselves with strong language. There is a large statue in downtown Helena dedicated to a bullwhacker cracking his whip.

Buffalo were nearing extinction in the entire country. They were mostly found in Montana, Texas, and Wyoming. The area below and above the forty-ninth parallel prospered in raining seasons but suffered during the dry seasons.

Rivers became difficult obstacles in the late 1800s, especially with snow in late spring and early fall, and the possibility of the chinook winds following right behind.

The railroads ruined river commerce. Fort Benton, on the Missouri River, was once the economic center for the Northern Plains until the railways arrived in the 1880s. The Great Northern RR was built in the area where Route 2 was constructed years later, known as the High Line. This was an open invitation to produce on the wide-open farmland.

We did, however, drive by two separate missile sites that were "at the ready" during the Cold

War. Finally, we found a hard highway, Route 200 where we had lunch at Big Sky Deli in Vaughn, Montana. This deli is a famous bakery that also serves as a restaurant. Our delicious sandwiches were made by Amish women. Mike did all the driving for five days with no complaints, even two hours on dirt roads, as Odessa and I were very appreciative.

Charlie Russell

That afternoon in Great Falls, we toured the Charles M. Russell museum, which included his log cabin studio plus his personal home. He had a collection of firearms in his log cabin as props. Many of them were designed by a contemporary, John Browning (1855–1926). Charles Russell (1864–1926) was self-taught but did spend two years in New York City in 1903–4 with experienced artists. He had an open-door policy while he painted. Women and Native Indians weren't allowed in saloons, but they were always welcomed at his studio. He was America's cowboy artist.

In the museum, there was an impressive collection of the Browning Firearms. Russell said, "Any man that can make a living doing what he likes is lucky, and I'm that. … To me the roar of a mountain stream mingled with the bells of a pack train is grander music than all the string or brass bands in the world."

There is a large painting of four Native American Indians sitting on their horses on a cliff overlooking the Missouri River. And it says beneath the painting: Russell's piece depicts an earlier moment as the Indians quietly watch a steamboat plying the Missouri.

Russell attended many rodeos, from those in his backyard of Montana—the Great Northern Stampede in Havre—to the roundups in Miles City and Bozeman to the big events in Pendleton and Calgary. It's clear that Russell enjoyed the aspects of the rodeo that most resembled the ones that took place on the open range, namely bronc riding and steer roping, activities that are prominently depicted in his paintings.

The appeal of Charlie's work was in the realism of the activities and the accuracy of the detail, as revealed in *Wakeup Time*, a watercolor showing a weary night wrangler coming off duty on a dreary, rainy morning.

Charlie's tiny 1887 sketch of a starving cow, *Waiting for a Chinook* (Montana Historical Society, Helena), was published in newspapers across the country to illustrate the loss of cattle that winter. His art career was thriving in 1888 as several stores in Helena were accepting his works, as were national magazines. This was the winter when my grandfather George Blake Bourne and James Edelin Hamilton (his stepbrother) started a sheep ranch, only to lose everything in the 1888 storm.

Our historical journey has now come to an end. Mike, Odessa, and I flew from Great Falls to our respective homes via Salt Lake City. It was thrilling for me to share this last trip with my wife and son to do research in the capital of the state about my father and grandfather. It was fitting that Mike was on the last trip, where we attended three games. I had coached him in every game of Little League, starting at age eight under the Fifty-Ninth Street Bridge on the East River in Manhattan. The baseball "diamond" was on an old red clay tennis court. And occasionally, debris would drop to our field of dreams from the bridge above.

At age thirteen, Mike moved upward to another level of the league, and I asked permission from the league to coach his team again. I reveled at his left-handed ability to pull sharp line drives down the right-field line. He was maturing into a real good hitter.

My wife had been vicariously sharing my experience of these trips since 1994. Her enthusiasm never waned throughout the years. It was fitting to have her with me on the last journey. But most of all, the three of us were together as a team for six days.

Sharing the drive through this open countryside with my wife and son gave me a deeper appreciation of the vastness and beauty of the fourth largest state. Most importantly, this was a similar trip that my grandfather took back in 1887, coming all the way from Washington, DC. It warmed my heart recalling the three of us gathering information in two libraries to research my father and grandfather. In effect, this is where my life started: in a newly built ranch house on the northern prairies of the Sweet Grass Hills between Chester, Montana, and the Canadian border.

My father was born in Helena, Montana, in 1903. I was born in Easton, Pennsylvania in 1936. My son Mike was born in Fort Worth, Texas, in 1976. Mike's biological parents gave Mike up for adoption, which afforded Odessa and me the opportunity to welcome him into our home at twenty-one days old. Mike and I had similar upbringings with our fathers. My father died when I was less than five years old. Mike's biological father departed at birth. In effect, neither one of us was raised by our respective natural-born fathers.

My mother remarried two years later to a good guy, Harold J. Lamm. And my son had me as his father. It has been a rewarding relationship, especially in the last several years. He took six days out of his busy work schedule to be with his mom and dad on this trip to the Northwest. I give a big hug to you, Michael Blake Bourne. I am so happy you are my son.

CHAPTER 17

ANALYTICS

• •

Vignettes of Baseball

Even though I barely received a passing grade of 65 in Statistics in my junior year of college, I am going to attempt to write about analytics. Why? Because all major sports, especially baseball, are now influenced by analytics. Statistics of all kinds are sliced and diced in different ways that end up on spreadsheets. *Money Ball*, the book written by Michael Lewis (2002) and later made into a movie, used concepts made by Bill James. These concepts helped Billy Beane's Oakland Athletics win 103 games and entry into the playoffs. This team had the sixth-smallest payroll in the league at that time.

Alan Roth

The Brooklyn Dodgers hired a statistician, Alan Roth, in 1949. He pushed the analysis of baseball statistics and was the first to be employed full time by a major league team. He would record virtually every pitch in a Dodger game for the next eighteen seasons. In the offseason, he would refine the numbers further, seeking longer-term trends and finding the outliers. Everyone knew left-handed hitters generally performed more poorly against left-handed pitchers and vice versa. Roth would look for, and find, the left-handed hitter who broke the mold and could provide a manager with an unexpected platoon advantage. He used spray charts showing the location of all of a player's batted balls. Today's TV announcers are all using this approach in 2019.

In 1954, Roth was moved into the radio booth to feed timely material to the Dodger announcers. The broadcast sponsors began to pay half of Roth's salary. Roth's major league debut was masked by Jackie Robinson's debut on the same day. Roth introduced the concept of the save in 1964. A few weeks later, he resigned and the team said it was because he was "tired of the travel."

In the 1960s he sat with Curt Gowdy and Tony Kubek on NBC for the *Game of the Week*. A few years later he moved to ABC to provide the same service, but ill health forced his retirement in the late 1980s, and he died in March 1992. Bill James said, "He was the guy who started it all. He took statisticians into a brave new world."

On-base percentage was more important to him than one's batting average. *Analytics* is just a fancy term for information. These stats can get very complicated and confusing. The analyst finds the nuances in numbers. And the average ballplayer has not shown the willingness to study and memorize them, with the exceptions being the catcher and pitcher.

In baseball, analytics track a player's tendencies, and the defensive alignment adjusts accordingly. There is a transfer of analytics from the iPad to the playing field. Every team now values advanced metrics.

Unexpected biases are now being discovered by artificial intelligence. Google recently unveiled a breakthrough artificial intelligence technology called BERT that changed the way scientists build systems that learn how people write and talk. BERT learned to identify the missing word or predict the next word in a sentence. Not surprisingly, fantasy baseball has always been looking for additional statistics. Specialists in analytics have not been invited into the broadcast booths, but maybe that day is coming.

Sig Mejdal

Here is a short history of a man who has influenced hundreds of players, dozens of coaches, minor league teams, and now three major league teams. Sig Mejdal, now age fifty-three, helped the St. Louis Cardinals make draft picks. He was an analyst with the Houston Astros, and now with the Baltimore Orioles as the assistant general manager. He comes with an impressive and unusual background to help the Orioles. He graduated from the University of California, Davis, with bachelor's degrees in mechanical engineering and aeronautical engineering. He received master's degrees in operations research and cognitive psychology from San Jose State University. During his teenage years, he was fascinated with the stats on the back of baseball cards. One of his jobs after college was a NASA researcher—engineer biomathematician.

He joined the Tri-City Valley Cats of Troy, New York, an affiliate of the Houston Astros as their development coach. It was a Class A team in the PONY League, and one of several teams that he advised. Manager Eneberg would consult Mejdal at least five times a game, asking what the numbers suggested in a given situation. He would ask his hitting and pitching coaches for their input, weigh his options, and then make a decision. Coach Mejdal would develop sophisticated reports on pitch usage and hitters' tendencies. He would highlight nuances of the game he had never noticed before: the footwork of catchers, the acceleration technique of base runners, and the drop back steps of outfielders. Possibly, he was experimenting with new strategies only in the minor leagues. However, he feels it is mandatory to have analytics.

Extra cameras were placed around most stadiums in the last two decades to help coaches analyze the opposing players from various angles. These cameras can even track the spin rate on a curveball. This would add to research reports upstairs in the baseball offices. These angles are not seen on TV. Teams are now tracking statistics of several thousand amateurs and several thousand professionals in the major and minor leagues.

Technology is a very helpful tool, but the athlete still must perform up to his ability. However, no stat is perfect. Does it give him an edge? Probably.

Below are a few humorous, brief, and true baseball stories:

1. Mark Twain, journalist and novelist, really wanted to play baseball. When relaxed, he talked baseball. He said, "I really prefer playing baseball to writing bestsellers. I lived for baseball, but once a coach told me, 'Don't come back for tryouts.'"

2. Tommy John of the New York Yankees recalled his 1974 arm surgery. "When the doctors operated, I told them to add in a Sandy Koufax fastball. They did but unfortunately it was Mrs. Koufax's."

3. Flatter seams on the baseball have less air resistance, known as drag-decrease. The stitches are compressed deeper into the leather of the ball, which makes it more difficult for the pitcher to deliver an effective split-finger pitch. The argument of juicing the ball continues as home runs for 2019 were a record 6,776 in the major leagues versus the last record of 6,105 in 2017. Players pulled 40.7 percent of their hits in 2019, implying they were going for round-trippers. Small ball baseball: singles, stolen bases, and bunts have all declined. Strikeouts continue to rise rapidly, as more hitters are going for home runs. The pitcher puts the index and middle finger on separate seams on opposite sides of the ball. There is an entire lace empty in between the two fingers. A split fastball sinks just as it approaches home plate, and the batter has already committed to swinging over the top of the ball. The pitcher uses the same motion as his fastball, which tricks the hitter. Bruce Sutter invented the pitch. Roger Craig was one of the first proponents as a player and manager from the 1950s to the 1980s. Masahiro Tanaka of the New York Yankees is presently striking hitters out with the splitter. However, fastballs were a record average of 93.1 miles per hour. So, it appears that it is still very difficult to hit a baseball.

4. Most players have a higher batting average with the bases loaded than any other time because the pitchers have to throw strikes. This also occurs when the infield is drawn in because of a runner at third base. Then batting averages in both situations go up fifty points.

5. Once, after striking out swinging at three bad pitches, Yogi Berra had the brass to ask indignantly, "How can a pitcher that wild stay in the league?"[7]

6. Driving in 1972 to Cooperstown, Dad took a wrong turn. Mom said, "Yogi, you're lost." He said, "Yeah, but we're making good time."

7 Baseball is a game where a curve is an optical illusion, a screwball can be a pitch or a person, stealing is legal, and you can spit anywhere you like except in the umpire's eye or on the ball.[8]

8. The Richmond, Indiana, Roosters baseball team, several years ago, had already washed fans'

[7] George Will, *Men at Work* (1990).
[8] Will, *Men at Work*.

clothes at Laundry Night but had to call off their latest promotion for legal reasons. A wet spring had helped cause an infestation of snakes in a Richmond neighborhood. So, the Roosters, a team in the independent Frontier League, offered free admission to any fan who caught a snake and deposited it in a box at the stadium's main gate. The snakes were to be relocated.

The problem was, state law prohibited the capture of wild animals without a proper permit. The team sponsored Snake Awareness Night instead.

9. Deion Sanders, nicknamed "Prime Time," had nine seasons as a part-time career as a major league baseball outfielder plus an NFL defensive back. He is the only individual to appear in both a Super Bowl and a World Series. My son, Mike, and I flew in 1989 and 1990 to see the Yankees play in several parks around the country. One weekend, we were in Milwaukee to see the Yankees and saw Deion Sanders do something highly unusual. He hit a line drive home run, rounded the bases, came into home plate, stopped a few inches away from the plate, bent over, and cleaned the plate by brushing off the dirt with his hands.

10. Yogi Berra was sitting in a pew at Larry Doby's funeral with Commissioner Fay Vincent, Phil Rizzuto, and Ralph Branca. Yogi leaned over in front of Vincent and said to Branca, "I will go to your funeral if you go to mine."

11. A pesky batter, after he had fouled off several pitches, stepped out of the batter's box and yelled to the pitcher, "I am not a Broadway producer, but show me everything you've got."

12. Moe Drabowsky collected the phone numbers of bullpens all over the major leagues and enjoyed lightening all the burden of boredom by calling bullpens in other cities. Imitating the voices of various coaches, he would order relievers hundreds of miles away to start warming up.[9] Moe was a pitcher in seventeen seasons for eight different teams in the American and National Leagues. In 1966, he set a still-standing World Series record for the Baltimore Orioles as a reliever by striking out eleven batters in one game against the Los Angeles Dodgers.

---

[9] Will, *Men at Work.*

CONCLUSION

Baseball is actually a refreshing realm of diversity. The games are like snowflakes. They are perishable, and no one is exactly like any other. But to see the diversities of snowflakes, you must look closely and carefully. Baseball, more than any other sport, is enjoyed by the knowledgeable.

Baseball is a sport for the literate. A game is an orderly experience—perhaps too orderly for the episodic mentalities of television babies. A baseball game is, like a sentence, a linear sequence; like a paragraph, it proceeds sequentially. But to enjoy it you have to be able to read it. Baseball requires baseball literacy.[10]

---

[10] Will, *Men at Work.*

AFTERWORD

As a finance major in college, I never dreamed of writing a book. In junior year, John Keyes, a classmate and friend, arranged an interview with Professor Frank O'Malley, a renowned English professor of over four decades. He was born in Clinton, Massachusetts, in 1911, graduated from Notre Dame in 1932, taught English for forty-one years, and lived on the campus until his death in 1974. Somehow, I passed the interview to take two semesters of his course "Modern Catholic Writers" in my senior year.

He conveyed to us a comprehension of life via reasoning and faith. His love of literature and writing was his message to us. Upon his arrival each morning in the classroom, he divested himself of coat and package and strolled to the window, where he paused for several minutes. We students were all mesmerized, waiting for his first words. He then would recite a quote from Kierkegaard, Jacques Maritain, Graham Greene, and many other scholars. This was a class that was so full of power even for just a little student in college like me. His lectures were unusual and deep and sometimes difficult for me to understand. But somehow, my exposure in this class did give me the confidence and courage later on to write this book. I thank all the people who inspired me to write about these journeys throughout the United States and Canada.

Special gratitude goes to my wife, Odessa, who was constantly encouraging me during the process.

It is disappointing we did not visit a few of the southern states. However, hot and humid weather in July and August was the deciding factor. The Savannah Bananas would have been a logical choice, as they had two sellout seasons in 2017 and 2018, or the Bull Durham team in North Carolina.

The minor leagues are like family. Here is an extreme example: a player, Norm Zauchin, chased down a foul ball near first base for the Birmingham Barons, crashed over the railing, and landed in the lap of a fan named Janet Mooney, whom he would marry two years later in Birmingham, Alabama.

The major leagues have finally agreed with the players to have a sixty-game season, starting July 23, 2020. A total of forty minor league teams had already been eliminated. Drafts have been shortened from forty rounds to five. As of July 1, 2020, Minor League Baseball's 140-game schedule has been canceled due to the COVID-19 pandemic. This decision definitely questions the future of 160 minor league teams and an estimated eight thousand players. Major league teams were responsible for paying the players and the coaches. The minor league teams made their revenues from sales at the concession stands plus tickets. COVID-19 is still on everyone's mind. We hope this is not the new normal.